tell me a ta

Moira Andrew

Acknowledgements

The author and publishers would like to give special thanks to the staff of Abertillery Primary School, Dinas Powys Infant School and Ogmore Centre Trust for their generous help and support during the production of *Tell me a Tale*. They would also like to thank the children for their enthusiastic co-operation and for their contributions of art and language work.

Thank you also to Hilary Ansell for generating the work on Diwali lamps on page 71 and to Claire Brammer, George McCaffery and Thomas McCaffery for making the Castle Clocks page 19, Origami Boats page 41, and Months of the Year headdresses page 59.

Letter Home (page 52)

First published in 2002 by BELAIR PUBLICATIONS LIMITED
Albert House, Apex Business Centre, Boscombe Road, Dunstable, Beds LU5 4RL

© 2002 Folens on behalf of the author Moira Andrew

Commissioning Editor: Karen McCaffery   Editor: Elizabeth Miles
Design: Jane Conway   Photography: Kelvin Freeman   Cover design: Duncan McTeer

Illustrators: Graham-Cameron Illustration: Bridget Dowty pp28–29, 34–35, 48–49; Zara Slattery pp54–55, 60–61; Kirsty Wilson pp20–21, 66–67; Linda Rogers Associates: Roger Fereday pp6–7; Sara Silcock p41; Simon Girling and Associates: Jenny Press pp14–15, 42–43.

Origami boat (page 41) designed by Sy Chen.

ISBN 0 94788 236 7

The cover photograph is taken from page 26.

Contents

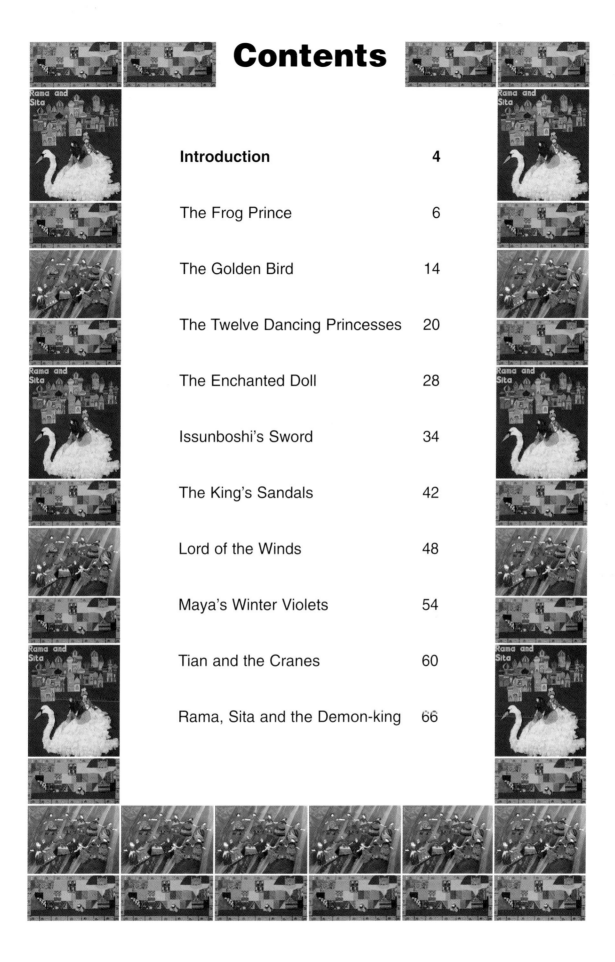

Introduction

Tell me a Tale is a collection of ten stories, some of which are well known, others less so. The first three tales, *The Frog Prince*, *The Golden Bird* and *The Twelve Dancing Princesses,* are adapted from the work of the Brothers Grimm. The rest are ancient stories from around the world (retold in modern language and idiom) that reflect different cultures and traditions.

The activities outlined in *Tell me a Tale* are intended as stimulus ideas for creative work. It is hoped that those who use the book will find their own ways of expressing their enjoyment of folktales through a variety of new and exciting ideas for follow-up work in writing and art.

Storytelling

Long before folktales were collected in books, stories were told and shared in homes and communities all around the world. In ancient times, many people were unable to read, so storytelling was an important part of their education and entertainment. By listening to songs and stories, people encountered amazing, magical worlds and learned how to overcome the difficulties and trials they might one day meet.

Before television and radio were invented, people often told one another stories around the fire, especially in the long winter evenings. These tales were seldom found in books, so they often changed shape as they were passed from one storyteller to another. A family who lived in a forest as woodcutters or charcoal-burners would tell the same story very differently from another family who had always been sheep-farmers living on hillsides or in valleys. Subjects that were important to one group were not always as important to another group. In this way, many different versions of a familiar story have evolved. Similarly, the version of each tale told in this book may be different again from those you may have read before.

The Brothers Grimm

Like many children, when the German brothers Jacob and Wilhelm Grimm were boys, they spent time listening to stories told to them by their mother and grandmother. They enjoyed these times so much that, when they grew up, they wrote the stories down, so that other people could read and share them. They gathered as many different versions of each tale as they could before writing them out in the form we see today. When the stories were finally published, they said, "We have added nothing of our own. We have written each tale more or less as it was told to us."

Hans Christian Andersen

Hans Christian Andersen, a Danish author, was a different kind of storyteller. He had a vivid imagination and invented his own stories, unlike the Brothers Grimm who simply listened and wrote down what they had heard. However, Hans Andersen very much admired the work of the Grimm Brothers and looked forward to meeting them. He once visited his heroes and was very hurt when he found out that they had never heard of him.

Folktale Traditions

There are similar traditions found in folktales from around the world. The language may be different, but many of the conventions remain the same. For example, 'three' is often a magic number, as in the familiar story, *The Three Bears*. In this book the magic 'three' is reflected in *Lord of the Winds* and *The Golden Bird*. A royal connection is another feature of many folktales, with the inclusion of kings and queens, princes and princesses.

Encourage children to think about such traditions and to look for links between stories from different countries and cultures. Many children enjoy researching folktales and the research can provide them with an interesting reason for further reading.

How to Use This Book

Tell me a Tale is designed to allow the teacher to read the stories aloud directly from the illustrated, double pages. These pages may also be photocopied, so that children can follow the text. The stories in *Tell me a Tale* make ideal starting points for language and artwork. Each story has four or more pages of follow-up activities and ideas, some of which are illustrated by display panels and photographs of children's work.

Display

Tell me a Tale illustrates a number of different ways in which children's work can be presented and displayed. Attractively mounted and displayed language and artwork delivers a message that children's work is valued and respected. Display should aim to develop children's thinking, celebrate their efforts and achievements and help to create an attractive and challenging classroom environment.

Moira Andrew

The Frog Prince

Once upon a time there was a king with seven lovely daughters. Each little girl was born even more beautiful than the last and the king and queen loved them all dearly. When the six eldest princesses married and went away, the youngest had no one to play with. She was often very lonely.

For her birthday, the king gave his youngest and most beautiful daughter a golden ball, as round and shiny as the sun itself. It was her favourite toy and she played with it for hours on end.

One day, the youngest and most beautiful princess went out to play ball in the palace garden. She threw her golden ball higher and higher in all directions. She threw it high over the sunflowers, the tallest flowers in the garden. She threw it into the topmost branches of a great oak tree. Each time, she caught it again. Then she threw it so high that it bounced off the palace roof. This time the little princess wasn't so lucky. She missed the golden ball as it flew past and it dropped with a plop into the middle of the deep dark pond.

She tried to get it back with a stick. She leaned over the pond as far as she dared, but the golden ball had disappeared. The youngest and most beautiful princess began to cry. Her tears dropped plip-plop into the deep dark waters of the pond.

Suddenly, a fat green frog poked his head out of the pond. "Croak," he said. "I'll get your ball back for you if you make me a solemn promise."

"Anything, anything," said the little princess. "If you find my golden ball, you can have anything you want, I promise."

"You must promise to let me eat from your plate and sleep in your bed. And when you wake in the morning, you must kiss me," said the frog.

"No problem," said the little princess, thinking to herself that the frog would never leave his deep dark pond. "I promise!"

So the fat green frog dived deep down and found the golden ball. He gave it to the little princess. Then he smiled a wide froggy smile, jumped out of the pond and said, "Now, take me to the dining room."

The princess was horrified. "But my father, the king, is giving a dinner party for my beautiful sisters and their princes tonight. I can't possibly bring a frog to the party!"

"But you promised!" said the frog, hopping up the palace steps beside her.

The little princess ran past the frog, upstairs into her bedroom, and cried and cried. Later, she dried her eyes, changed into her party dress and tiptoed to her father's side at the long dining table. It was set with splendid golden knives and forks, silver candlesticks and great bowls of fruit. All the guests were dressed in their best, and the king and queen were very proud indeed of their seven beautiful daughters. There was a lot of noise as the guests laughed and talked together.

The king's servants were just putting a golden plate in front of each guest when there was a knock at the door. Everyone fell silent as a

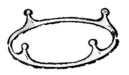

croaking voice asked to speak to the king's youngest and most beautiful daughter. There in the doorway, sat the fat green frog.

"You can't possibly come in here," hissed the princess. "But you promised," said the frog and jumped up to sit at the table between the princess's golden knife and fork. He smiled up at her with his wide froggy smile. "You promised I could eat from your plate," he said. Nobody moved. Nobody spoke.

The princess screamed, "Get away! I can't possibly share my dinner with a frog."

"Did you promise, my little princess?" asked her father, the king.

"Yes," she whispered.

"Then you must keep your promise," said the king and he told his servants to bring an extra helping of food for the frog.

"Thank you, your majesty," said the frog and he began to eat his dinner from the golden plate.

When he had finished, the frog yawned a wide froggy yawn. "Time for bed," he said.

He hopped upstairs behind the little princess and jumped on her bed. The princess began to cry. "You can't sleep here," she sobbed.

"But you promised!" said the frog. So the little princess made room for him on her pillow, turned her back and cried herself to sleep.

Next morning, the little princess found the frog was still sitting on her pillow. He smiled his wide froggy smile and put his fat green face up to her mouth. "I'm waiting to be kissed," he said.

"No way!" said the princess and she jumped out of bed. The frog followed her. "But you promised!" he said.

Outside her bedroom they met the king in his purple dressing gown. "Did you promise, my little princess?" he asked.

"Yes," she whispered.

"Then you must keep your promise," said the king.

So the youngest and most beautiful princess held her nose, screwed up her eyes and kissed the frog, smack, on his wide green mouth. Suddenly, the frog disappeared and the world's most handsome prince stood in his place.

"I have been under a spell," he said. "Only a kiss from a beautiful princess could break it. You kissed me, so here I am!"

The prince was so handsome that the youngest and most beautiful princess felt like kissing him again, but before she could do so, the prince asked her to marry him.

"Yes, yes," she said. "And I will promise to love you forever."

They were married the next day and there was rejoicing throughout the land. All the king's beautiful daughters came to the wedding, but the bride, the youngest daughter, was the most beautiful of all.

The Frog Prince

Speaking and Listening

- Listen to this folktale read aloud. *The Frog Prince* is one of a collection of fairy stories gathered and retold by the German brothers, Jacob and Wilhelm Grimm. How many different versions of *The Frog Prince* story can you find?

Favourite Toys

- The princess in the story had a golden ball, 'It was her favourite toy and she played with it for hours on end.' Talk about favourite toys and compare which toys boys/girls like best.

Promises

- Discuss what it means 'to make a promise'. Why do you think the king told the little princess, 'You must keep your promise'? Talk about promises that you might make at home, for example, keeping your bedroom tidy. Discuss and write out a list of ten promises that might help to make the classroom or playground a happier place.

- Children who are members of a club often make promises when they join. Ask anyone who has made 'a solemn promise' (Brownies, Scouts, Beavers, etc.) what kind of things they have promised to do or not to do.

- If children have a secret society, perhaps in the garden shed, discuss with them the kind of promises they would put in the rules and get other members to keep.

Loneliness

- Think about the little princess: 'She had no one to play with. She was often very lonely.' Talk about occasions when, like the princess, you feel lonely. Consider the kinds of games that you play on your own. How do they differ from those you can play with others? Talk about how important friends might be to children who don't have brothers or sisters to play with.

- Think about other people who might be lonely for other reasons, for example, grandmas and grandads who live alone. Discuss ways in which you might be able to help, by visiting them perhaps, or sending a letter or card.

Language Activities

Hunt the Adjectives

- Photocopy the story, then read it through and underline every adjective in red (examples: beautiful, golden, favourite). Working collaboratively, rewrite the story, replacing the adjectives with new ones. Discuss the finished version and talk about what difference (if any) the changes have made to the narrative.

Magic Haiku

- A haiku is a Japanese form of verse which uses three lines. There are five syllables in the first line, seven in the second and five in the third, for example 'Wave a magic wand' has five beats and would make an excellent first (or last) line.

- Write the magic spell for turning the prince into a frog as a haiku. For example:

Wave a magic wand!(5)
Make the prince a fat green frog.(7)
Wake him with a kiss.(5)

- Scribe your spell on a silver star at the top of a magic wand.

- Read the poem, 'The Witch's Brew' (from *The Witch's Brew* by Wes Magee, Cambridge 1989) for more spell-making ideas. Put your magic spell poems on a witch's hat or write them out on the wings of a black bat.

Lifecycle of a Frog

- Write a four-page zigzag book tracing the lifecycle of the frog. Make this an illustrated factual account.

Portrait of a Frog

- Contrast the factual account of the lifecycle of a frog with a poem that uses images to express the characteristics of a frog.

- Make up images to describe the sound of the frog's croak, the look of his wide mouth, the feel of his skin and so on. Use your list of images to make a portrait of a frog in words.

I was a Frog!

- You are a reporter for the local newspaper. You hear about the prince who used to be a frog and rush off to get his story. Invite him to 'tell the story in his own words' and make it into a sensational report. Find a catchy headline to go with it, for example: *FROG DRAMA PRINCE SPEAKS OUT, KISS FROM A PRINCESS, KING'S DAUGHTER WEDS FROG PRINCE.*

Postcard from the Palace

- Imagine that you are a guest at the king's dinner party. Write a postcard home to tell your mum/dad/friend what happened. Remember, there isn't a lot of space on a postcard, so you must write concisely. Draw and colour a picture of the palace on the front of your postcard.

Play Script

- Rewrite the story as a play script. There are several decisions to make before you work on the dialogue.

  1. You need a list of characters. The principal ones are the Princess, the King and the Frog Prince. You may wish to add other characters so that more children can take part, for example, Queen, Party Guests, Pageboy, Butler, Nanny and so on.

  2. Describe the setting (where the scene is taking place), for example:

     Scene 1:   Inside the palace OR In the tower OR In the palace garden ...

  3. Give stage directions that show what the characters do, their entrances and exits (coming and going) and how each is feeling, for example, bored, excited, tired and so on.

  4. Work on the dialogue, some of which is given in the story, but you may need to invent more conversation.

     For example:

     Scene 1:   Inside the palace. A beautiful young girl wanders about, looking bored.

     Princess: I wish I had someone to play with. I'm lonely all by myself.

The Toad Princess

- Imagine that the story is told with a young prince as the hero. Turn the king into a queen and the frog into a different creature of your choice, such as a lizard, toad or goldfish. Only a kiss from the prince can turn the creature into a beautiful princess. You might also want to bring your story up to date, describing princes riding around the palace gardens on silver scooters or skateboards. Illustrate your finished story.

Art Activities

The King's Party

- Make a display panel of the king's party showing a long table set out with plates and glasses, bowls of fruit and so on. Add candles to make the setting look very grand. Behind the table seat the guests, with the king and the princess in the middle and immediately in front of them a large green spotted frog. Use paints or make it a collage piece.

Make a Pond Mobile

- Make a pond mobile by cutting out frog, toad, fish and water snail shapes from card. Attach to a hoop using nylon thread and suspend from the ceiling. Add strips of green weed, and waterlily leaves and flowers made from tissue or crêpe paper. Make dragonflies from silver paper, with Cellophane wings. Put these on wires and 'fly' them over the pond hoop.

Frog in the Pond

- Using a damp cloth, wet a piece of white paper. Then wipe streaks of blue and green paint across it and leave to dry. Once dry, cut the paper into a pond-shape. Paint lots of swimming frogs on another piece of paper, cut them out and glue them onto the pond. Decorate around the pond with a collage of stones and weeds.

A Lifecycle Wheel

- Make a lifecycle wheel by cutting out two circles of card the size of a tea-plate. On one plate draw diagrams showing the stages of the frog's lifecycle from spawn to adult frog. Colour and decorate the second circle to be like a pond, and add underwater weeds and waterlilies. Then cut out a viewing triangle and cover the inside with clingfilm to make it look like water. Fix the two circles with a paper fastener and revolve the top circle to reveal the stages in the frog's lifecycle.

Frog-prince Mask

- Design and make a mask for the frog prince to use in your play (see Language Activities). Cut out two matching frog-face shapes, large enough to cover your face. Cut out eye and mouth holes through both pieces of card. Use felt-tipped pens to make the frog's 'fat green face' on the front of the mask, giving him a 'wide froggy smile' Glue the two pieces of card back-to-back with a stick between them so that the mask can be held in front of the face.

Sock Puppets

- Make a sock puppet for each of the characters in the story. For each you will need a sock, an oval of card, glue and odds and ends of wool, bits of cloth, gold card, buttons or a broken necklace. Cut an oval of card to fit inside the sock and fold it over. Next, turn the sock inside out. Put glue on the inside fold of the oval card and press the toe of the sock into it. When the glue is dry, turn the sock the right way round and pull it over the card until it makes a smiling mouth. Add button eyes and wool hair, to decorate each character. The princess might have yellow wool hair and a little gold circlet. The frog should be green with spots. When he becomes the handsome prince, substitute the second green sock, decorated with a little crown.

The Golden Bird

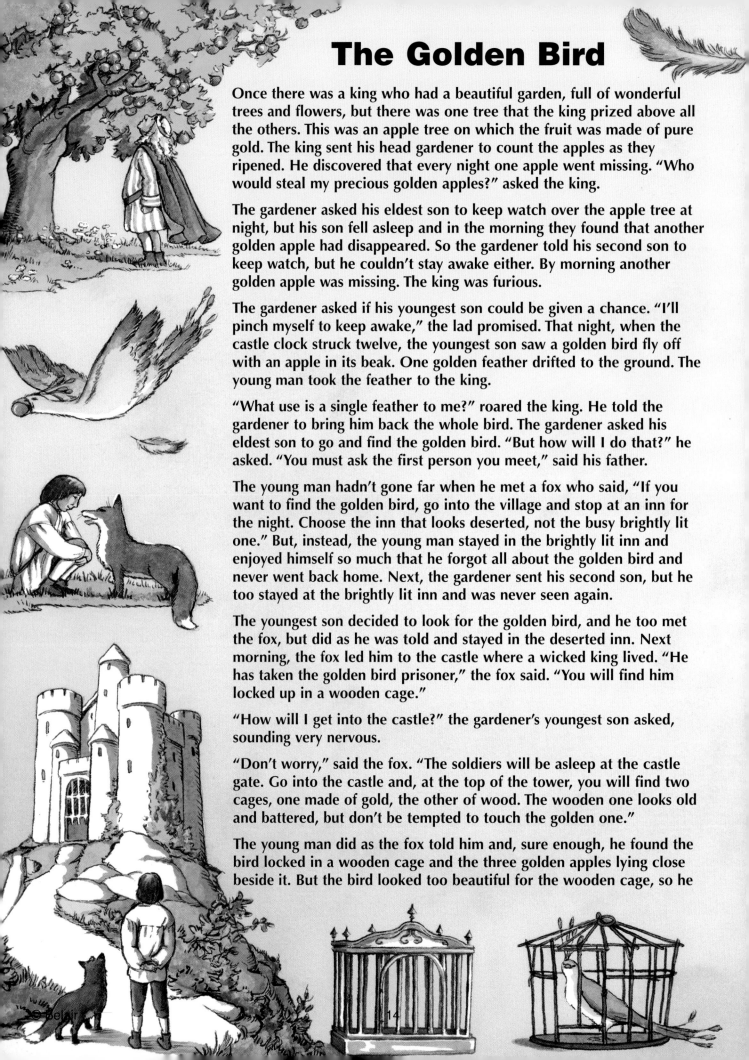

Once there was a king who had a beautiful garden, full of wonderful trees and flowers, but there was one tree that the king prized above all the others. This was an apple tree on which the fruit was made of pure gold. The king sent his head gardener to count the apples as they ripened. He discovered that every night one apple went missing. "Who would steal my precious golden apples?" asked the king.

The gardener asked his eldest son to keep watch over the apple tree at night, but his son fell asleep and in the morning they found that another golden apple had disappeared. So the gardener told his second son to keep watch, but he couldn't stay awake either. By morning another golden apple was missing. The king was furious.

The gardener asked if his youngest son could be given a chance. "I'll pinch myself to keep awake," the lad promised. That night, when the castle clock struck twelve, the youngest son saw a golden bird fly off with an apple in its beak. One golden feather drifted to the ground. The young man took the feather to the king.

"What use is a single feather to me?" roared the king. He told the gardener to bring him back the whole bird. The gardener asked his eldest son to go and find the golden bird. "But how will I do that?" he asked. "You must ask the first person you meet," said his father.

The young man hadn't gone far when he met a fox who said, "If you want to find the golden bird, go into the village and stop at an inn for the night. Choose the inn that looks deserted, not the busy brightly lit one." But, instead, the young man stayed in the brightly lit inn and enjoyed himself so much that he forgot all about the golden bird and never went back home. Next, the gardener sent his second son, but he too stayed at the brightly lit inn and was never seen again.

The youngest son decided to look for the golden bird, and he too met the fox, but did as he was told and stayed in the deserted inn. Next morning, the fox led him to the castle where a wicked king lived. "He has taken the golden bird prisoner," the fox said. "You will find him locked up in a wooden cage."

"How will I get into the castle?" the gardener's youngest son asked, sounding very nervous.

"Don't worry," said the fox. "The soldiers will be asleep at the castle gate. Go into the castle and, at the top of the tower, you will find two cages, one made of gold, the other of wood. The wooden one looks old and battered, but don't be tempted to touch the golden one."

The young man did as the fox told him and, sure enough, he found the bird locked in a wooden cage and the three golden apples lying close beside it. But the bird looked too beautiful for the wooden cage, so he

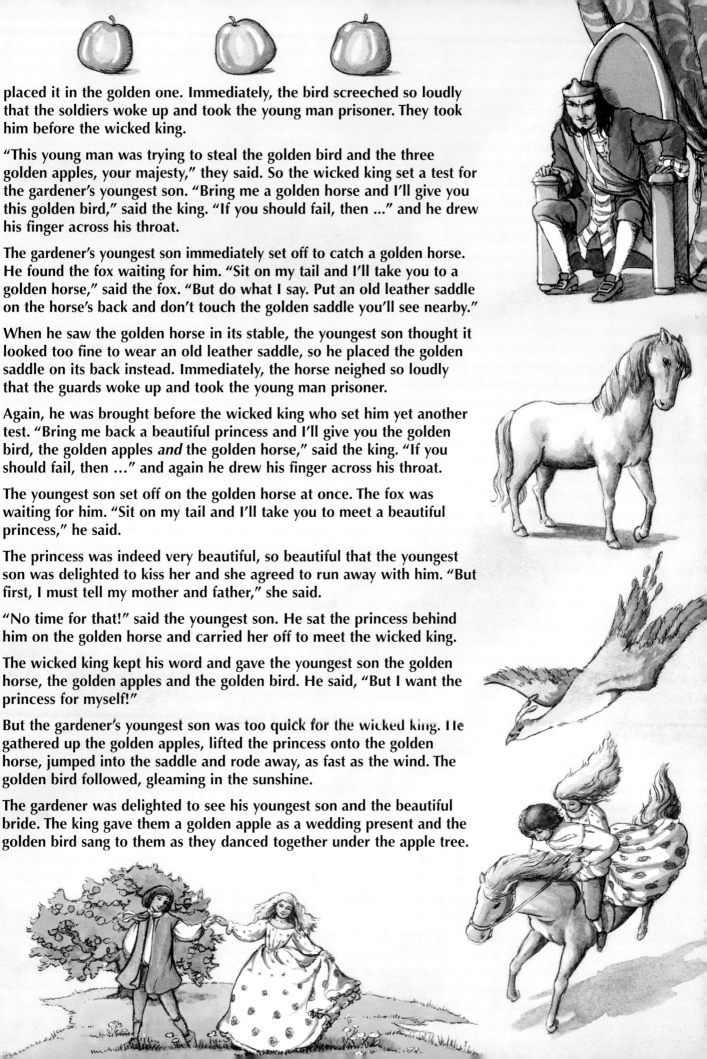

placed it in the golden one. Immediately, the bird screeched so loudly that the soldiers woke up and took the young man prisoner. They took him before the wicked king.

"This young man was trying to steal the golden bird and the three golden apples, your majesty," they said. So the wicked king set a test for the gardener's youngest son. "Bring me a golden horse and I'll give you this golden bird," said the king. "If you should fail, then ..." and he drew his finger across his throat.

The gardener's youngest son immediately set off to catch a golden horse. He found the fox waiting for him. "Sit on my tail and I'll take you to a golden horse," said the fox. "But do what I say. Put an old leather saddle on the horse's back and don't touch the golden saddle you'll see nearby."

When he saw the golden horse in its stable, the youngest son thought it looked too fine to wear an old leather saddle, so he placed the golden saddle on its back instead. Immediately, the horse neighed so loudly that the guards woke up and took the young man prisoner.

Again, he was brought before the wicked king who set him yet another test. "Bring me back a beautiful princess and I'll give you the golden bird, the golden apples *and* the golden horse," said the king. "If you should fail, then ..." and again he drew his finger across his throat.

The youngest son set off on the golden horse at once. The fox was waiting for him. "Sit on my tail and I'll take you to meet a beautiful princess," he said.

The princess was indeed very beautiful, so beautiful that the youngest son was delighted to kiss her and she agreed to run away with him. "But first, I must tell my mother and father," she said.

"No time for that!" said the youngest son. He sat the princess behind him on the golden horse and carried her off to meet the wicked king.

The wicked king kept his word and gave the youngest son the golden horse, the golden apples and the golden bird. He said, "But I want the princess for myself!"

But the gardener's youngest son was too quick for the wicked king. He gathered up the golden apples, lifted the princess onto the golden horse, jumped into the saddle and rode away, as fast as the wind. The golden bird followed, gleaming in the sunshine.

The gardener was delighted to see his youngest son and the beautiful bride. The king gave them a golden apple as a wedding present and the golden bird sang to them as they danced together under the apple tree.

The Golden Bird

Speaking and Listening

- Listen to the story *The Golden Bird* read aloud or take a copy and read it silently. *The Golden Bird* is one of the less well-known folktales in the Brothers Grimm collection. However, it is full of features that we read about again and again in fairy stories.

- When we get to the end of many traditional stories, we usually find that the characters 'live happily ever after'. *The Golden Bird* is a tale in which the hero has to perform a number of almost impossible tasks before he marries the princess. Often the heroes and heroines in fairytales have to be very brave. Can you find other stories with a main character who is courageous?

- Look for other familiar fairytale traditions in the story of *The Golden Bird*, for example, a king, three sons and the promise of lots of gold.

- Predict part of the story. Read the first two paragraphs and then consider who might have stolen the king's golden apples.

- Listen to other stories which have different fairytale traditions, for example, promises, wishes, fairy godmothers or giants, witches and elves. You might suggest *Jack and the Beanstalk, Cinderella* or *The Elves and the Shoemaker*.

Golden Apples

- In *The Golden Bird* we hear that the king prized one tree over everything else that grew in his wonderful garden. It was 'an apple tree on which the fruit was made of pure gold'. Think about this idea and discuss the good and bad things about a tree laden with golden fruit. You could sell the golden apples, but they wouldn't be much good to you if you were feeling hungry! Write out your conclusions about gold fruit as two lists, labelled 'for' and 'against'.

Following Instructions

- What did the fox tell the young men to do? What happened to them when they disobeyed? Talk about the times when it is important to follow instructions (when you are crossing roads, on school trips and so on) and when it might be more important to think for yourself.

Language Activities

Shape Poem

- Look for different images to describe the golden apples. What do they look like? What do they make you think of? Encourage the children to use imaginative comparisons, so that they begin to use images or similes (which form the cornerstone of poetry). Each phrase should begin 'like a ...', so a golden apple is described as being like a shiny star, like a full moon, like a traffic light and so on. Scribe the images along the branches of a tree. Hang golden apples around the tree and draw or add cut-out green leaves.

Silver Strawberries

- Retell the story in your own words, replacing the golden apples with a different kind of fruit, such as silver strawberries. You might also substitute a queen for the king, three daughters for the gardener's sons and a different animal for the fox. Follow the structure of the original story, but make lots of changes along the way and see what happens.

The Golden Bird

- Look at a variety of information books on birds and list some of the things that the author thinks are important, for example: size, colour, wingspan, habitat, food, mating displays and eggs. Look for diagrams and photographs of birds in flight, their nests, feeding habits and so on. Make a pamphlet about the imaginary 'golden bird' following the structure of the information books.

Cartoon Characters

- Create a cartoon strip telling the story of *The Golden Bird*. Work on the dialogue so that everyone in the story has words to say. Some of the dialogue is already there, such as, when the fox says, 'Sit on my tail and I'll take you to a golden horse.' Draw the story as a comic strip with the characters' words written inside speech bubbles.

If You Should Fail

- Twice in the story, the wicked king threatens the youngest son with the words, "If you should fail, then ..." but each time the young man disappears before the king can finish his sentence. Suggest the fate that might befall him, remembering that *The Golden Bird* is a folktale where people are changed into animals or put to sleep for a thousand years! Make up a set of the wicked king's threats and show them correctly written inside speech marks.

The Youngest Son's Diary

- Write a few pages of the youngest son's diary from the moment he sets off to find the golden bird until his meeting with the beautiful princess. Include how he felt about things and describe what he saw on the way. For example:

August

23 Wednesday

My brothers are still missing. Went to tell my Dad that I'd try my luck. Set out to look for the golden bird.

Met a fox with a bushy brown tail. He seemed to know all about me. "Don't stay at the inn where all the lights are blazing," he told me. "Go to the one across the road."

August

Thursday **24**

Up bright and early.

The fox was waiting to give me my instructions for the day. "Jump up," he said and rode off with me clinging to his back. Came to a castle on a hill. "The wicked king lives there," the fox said. I was absolutely terrified. "How do I get in?" I asked.

- Look at the informal writing used for a diary entry. Notice how, for example, it is not always written in complete sentences. Often the 'I' is left out. Compile the diary into a zigzag book format and illustrate. Alternatively, work in a group and give the children a page each suggesting that they write up one page for one day. Use the word-processor to present the finished work and paint pictures to go with it. Display as a wall story.

18

Art Activities

The Castle Clock

- The story tells us that when 'the castle clock struck twelve, the youngest son saw a golden bird fly off with an apple in its beak'. Design a clock fit for a castle wall using card and coloured paper. Cut out a large circle from coloured card. On bright contrasting paper, and a piece of tracing paper, cut out a smaller circle. Fold the tracing paper into quarters, then into thirds by bending both edges in so that they overlap. Draw a line about 4 centimetres from the edge and make a mark halfway along this line. Cut in from both corners. Unfold the tracing paper to give a star shape with 12 points. Trace this outline on to the paper circle and cut it out. Glue to the coloured card circle. Add the numbers 1 to 12 at the points of the star. (You might like to use Roman numerals.) Decorate the clock, perhaps putting a sun and moon face in the middle. Add hands pointing to 12 o'clock.

The Beautiful Garden

- Make a wall display of the king's beautiful garden ('full of wonderful trees and flowers'), collage-style with painted and cut-out flowers. Glue 'flying' butterflies and dragonflies on the skyline. Using gold foil for the apples, place a tree with a crop of golden apples in the middle of the picture. Finish off with the golden bird flying high above the garden.

Golden Apples

- Make apples using salt dough, and add a stalk and a leaf. Bake at a low heat in the oven for about 1 hour. Dry out for a day before spraying with gold paint.

The Twelve Dancing Princesses

Once there was a king with twelve beautiful daughters. He loved them all dearly, but was very puzzled by what happened every night when they were supposed to be asleep. All the princesses slept in one big bedroom. Every evening, the king kissed them goodnight and then locked their bedroom door, but every morning the princesses' satin shoes were worn through and full of holes.

"What has happened to your pretty shoes? Were you dancing last night when you should have been sleeping?" asked the king each morning.

"No, father," they said. "We slept until sunrise." But the king didn't believe them. He sent word around his kingdom that any man who discovered where the princesses went each night could choose one of them for his wife. "But each of you only has three days to find out," said the king.

When the young men of the kingdom heard the news, hundreds of them queued around the palace walls, each hoping to try his luck. The king invited each in turn to sleep in the room next to the princesses' bedroom and watch what happened. However, the eldest princess always offered them a glass of sweet wine. As soon as the wine touched their lips, all the young men fell into a deep sleep and didn't wake again till morning. Every morning, just as before, twelve pairs of dancing shoes full of holes were tossed aside on the princesses' bedroom floor. The king was very puzzled and extremely cross. "What more can we do?" he asked the queen in despair.

A poor soldier set off to the palace to try his luck. On his way, he met an old beggar woman and gave her a penny. "I'd like to give you more," he said, "but this is all I've got." He showed her his empty pockets.

"Where are you going, kind sir?" she asked.

"I'm off to the palace to find out where the princesses go each night," said the soldier. "Perhaps I'll be lucky."

"It won't be difficult," said the old woman. "But don't drink the wine these beautiful princesses will offer you. Just pretend to drink it and then pretend to fall asleep." She gave him an invisible cloak to wear. "Wear this cloak", she said, "and you'll be able to follow them wherever they go."

When the soldier arrived at the palace, the king took him to meet his daughters. As soon as the king had kissed them goodnight, the princesses offered the soldier a glass of sweet wine, which he pretended to drink, then he lay on the floor and pretended to sleep.

He watched enchanted as the princesses dressed in their finest ball gowns of silk and satin and lace. They put ribbons in their hair and pretty satin shoes on their feet. The eldest princess tapped the floor beside her bed and suddenly a trapdoor opened. From it, a long staircase led down into the darkness. One by one, the princesses disappeared down the stairs. They laughed and whispered excitedly to one another.

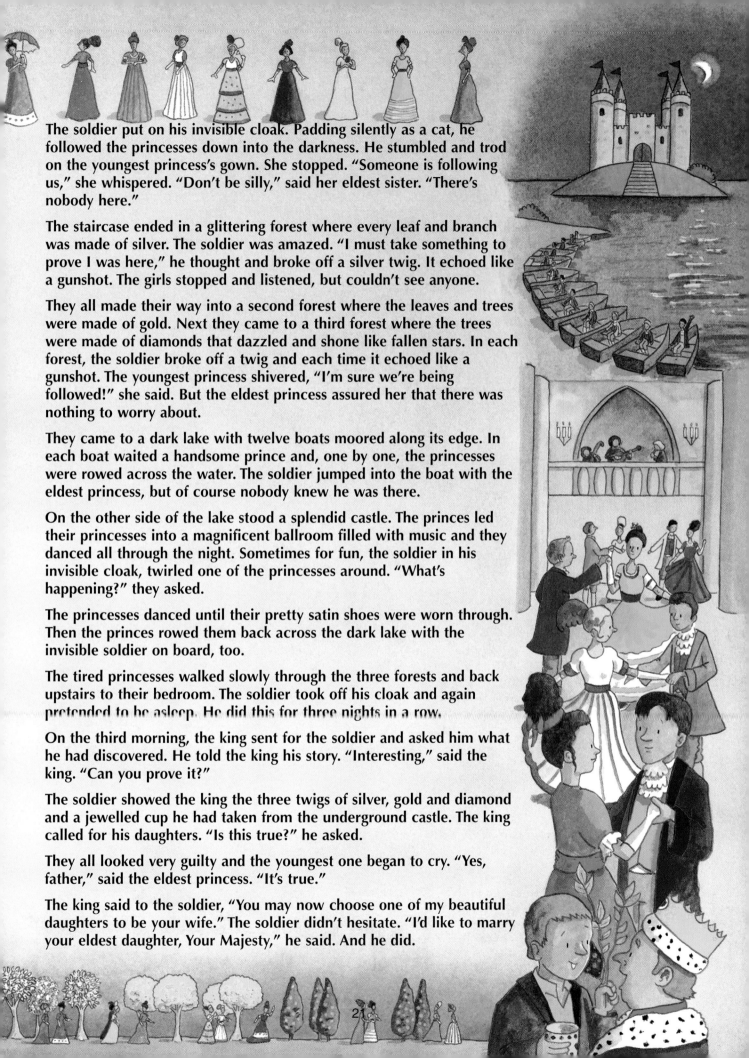

The soldier put on his invisible cloak. Padding silently as a cat, he followed the princesses down into the darkness. He stumbled and trod on the youngest princess's gown. She stopped. "Someone is following us," she whispered. "Don't be silly," said her eldest sister. "There's nobody here."

The staircase ended in a glittering forest where every leaf and branch was made of silver. The soldier was amazed. "I must take something to prove I was here," he thought and broke off a silver twig. It echoed like a gunshot. The girls stopped and listened, but couldn't see anyone.

They all made their way into a second forest where the leaves and trees were made of gold. Next they came to a third forest where the trees were made of diamonds that dazzled and shone like fallen stars. In each forest, the soldier broke off a twig and each time it echoed like a gunshot. The youngest princess shivered, "I'm sure we're being followed!" she said. But the eldest princess assured her that there was nothing to worry about.

They came to a dark lake with twelve boats moored along its edge. In each boat waited a handsome prince and, one by one, the princesses were rowed across the water. The soldier jumped into the boat with the eldest princess, but of course nobody knew he was there.

On the other side of the lake stood a splendid castle. The princes led their princesses into a magnificent ballroom filled with music and they danced all through the night. Sometimes for fun, the soldier in his invisible cloak, twirled one of the princesses around. "What's happening?" they asked.

The princesses danced until their pretty satin shoes were worn through. Then the princes rowed them back across the dark lake with the invisible soldier on board, too.

The tired princesses walked slowly through the three forests and back upstairs to their bedroom. The soldier took off his cloak and again pretended to be asleep. He did this for three nights in a row.

On the third morning, the king sent for the soldier and asked him what he had discovered. He told the king his story. "Interesting," said the king. "Can you prove it?"

The soldier showed the king the three twigs of silver, gold and diamond and a jewelled cup he had taken from the underground castle. The king called for his daughters. "Is this true?" he asked.

They all looked very guilty and the youngest one began to cry. "Yes, father," said the eldest princess. "It's true."

The king said to the soldier, "You may now choose one of my beautiful daughters to be your wife." The soldier didn't hesitate. "I'd like to marry your eldest daughter, Your Majesty," he said. And he did.

The Twelve Dancing Princesses

Speaking and Listening

- Listen to the story of *The Twelve Dancing Princesses*. This story comes from the Grimm Brothers' collection of folktales.

- Princesses are a favourite character of fairy folktales. Can you think of other fairy stories about a princess?

Magic Numbers

- In many fairytales three is a familiar number. In this story anyone who can discover where the princesses go each night has 'only three days to find out'. Where else in the story is the number three important?

Being Invisible

- When the old woman met the soldier in the story, 'she gave him an invisible coat to wear'. Talk about some of the things you might be able to do if you had an invisible cloak. Discuss the good and bad possibilities.

Precious Jewels

- The staircase ended in a forest 'where every leaf and branch was made of silver'. The next forest was made of gold and the third of diamonds. Can you think of other jewels to make a different magic forest? What would a ruby forest look like? Or an emerald one?

Sparkling Leaves

- Make a thesaurus of verbs to describe how the gold and silver leaves sparkle in the glittering forests (gleams, sparkles, twinkles). Display the words on glittering leaf shapes and attach to a golden tree.

Telling Lies

- In *The Twelve Dancing Princesses* what do the girls say to their father, the king? Do they tell the truth? Talk about how important it is to tell the truth.

Language Activities

Twelve Pretty Princesses

- Make up a number poem, beginning at twelve and working downwards, about the twelve princesses.
  For example:

> **Twelve** pretty princesses dancing down the stair.
>   **Eleven** pretty princesses putting flowers in their hair.
>   **Ten** pretty princesses twirling round and round.
>   **Nine** pretty princesses making not a sound.

> **Twelve** handsome princes rowing across the lake.
>   **Eleven** handsome princes enjoying a slice of cake.
>   **Ten** handsome princes sailing in a boat.
>   **Nine** handsome princes each in a velvet coat.

- Try to write in rhyming couplets, that is, first and second lines rhyming, third and fourth and so on. Alternatively, you could write a similar poem about the princes.

- You could write out your finished poems on a staircase background, emphasising the number at the beginning of each new line.

- Write a new number poem with different storybook characters, for example, 'Twelve Wicked Wizards' or 'Twelve Hairy Hobbits'.

The Magic Forest

- Use some of the 'sparkling' verbs to create poetic images of the magic shining trees. Work collaboratively, each child contributing ideas. Write the poems on black paper with silver or gold pens and display against gold or silver backing paper.

The magic forest
  shimmers
like stars in a winter sky,
  glitters
like a waterfall in the sun,
  flashes
like a dragonfly's wings …

In a Modern Setting

- Bring the story *The Twelve Dancing Princesses* up to date. Describe the princes and princesses as boys and girls of today. *The Twelve Disco Kids* might make a good title. Send them off to dance to a beat band, revolving disco lights replacing the glitter of the magic forests.

What Have You Been Doing?

- Compose a variety of different explanations or lies that the twelve dancing princesses could give their father the king when, each morning, he asked: "What has happened to your pretty shoes?"

Through the Trapdoor

- In the story it says, 'suddenly a trapdoor opened ...' and the princesses found a long staircase leading to a silver forest. Imagine what else might lie behind a magic trapdoor – a summer garden? a tropical island? an underwater world? Write a poem called 'Through the Trapdoor', listing all the magical things you might find if you tapped your bedroom floor 'and suddenly a trapdoor opened'. Display the finished poem beneath an opening door.

The Invisible Cloak

- Write an adventure story about a day in your life when you get to wear an invisible cloak. Think about the things you could do or the places you could go.

Art Activities

The Deep Dark Lake

● Make a display panel of the dark lake with the castle silhouetted against a starry sky. Paint the lake in purple. Add a great golden moon and twinkling stars against the night sky. Along the edge of the lake, show the magic forest with shiny coloured leaves and tall grasses. You could add twelve cut-out boats arranged as though they are sailing across the lake.

Enchanted Castle

● Use a variety of empty boxes to build a model of the enchanted castle where the princesses danced all night. Give the castle high towers made from tubes of card and paint each of the windows yellow, as though lights were blazing in every room. Surround the castle with a lake made from crumpled blue foil paper and blue and green Cellophane. Add pebbles to make a beach. To finish off the model, place twelve black rowing boats made from card on the Cellophane waves. Tie them to the base of the castle with string, as if they are moored on the edge of the lake.

Dancing Paper Princesses

- Fold a long strip of paper into twelve. On the top fold, draw the outline of a princess wearing a ball gown. Draw the hands outstretched to touch the edge of the fold. Cut out through all twelve folds, making sure that the hand section is still intact. Unfold to show twelve princesses dancing hand-in-hand. Paint or use felt-tipped pens to show each ball gown in a different colour.

Design an Invisible Cloak

- The old woman gave the soldier an invisible cloak to wear. Design an invisible cloak, using a white wax crayon on white paper. Draw the outline shape, then fill in the cloak with squiggly patterns. The cloak will be invisible until you cover it with a wash of thin coloured paint.

The Princesses' Bedroom

- Use offcuts of striped wallpaper or make a striped background using gold, silver and coloured pens. Cut out twelve beds and position them against the wall. Glue on scraps of coloured material to look like quilts. At the end of each bed, place a pair of cut-out slippers with a jewel, made from a sequin, pasted on the toe of each.

Sparkling Leaves

- Make a glittering forest display by cutting out large leaves from foil paper. Decorate the leaves with glitter, beads and sequins to make them sparkle. Display them on silver, gold and diamond trees.

The Enchanted Doll

Tirawa had five brothers. They lived with their mother and father in a pine forest, where a blue river ran wide and deep and purple mountains reached for the sky. Although Tirawa was the youngest, he could do most things better than any of his brothers. He could run faster, climb higher and shoot further. Worst of all, as far as the brothers were concerned, Tirawa could hunt better than any of them. They were very jealous. Sometimes they played horrible tricks on Tirawa. Sometimes they called him names and bullied him.

One morning, when he could stand their cruelty no longer, Tirawa decided to join a new tribe, far from the mountains and the pine forest and the wide blue river. He put on a new pair of leather moccasins that his mother had made for him. Tirawa was very proud of these special leather moccasins, which were so soft that animals couldn't hear him coming when he went hunting. Tirawa said goodbye to his mother and father and went out into the forest. He felt very sad as he walked away from the tall purple mountains that he had known all his life.

He hadn't gone far when he met a strange old man. "Please sir, can you tell me where this path goes?" Tirawa asked.

"It leads to the next village," said the old man. "But you will need to take great care. The way is very steep and the path is rough and covered with sharp stones. It's just as well that you have such a beautiful pair of leather moccasins on your feet."

"My mother made them for me," Tirawa said proudly.

Just then, Tirawa noticed that the old man was limping badly. "My feet are very painful," he said. So Tirawa took off his soft leather moccasins and gave them to the old man. The old man smiled and put them on his poor sore feet.

"Thank you, my child," he said. "You are very kind, so I'm going to give you a present. Take good care of it." He gave Tirawa a little wooden box and then, quite suddenly, disappeared.

Tirawa wondered where the old man had gone. He looked everywhere, but the old man was nowhere to be seen. "He must have magic powers," Tirawa thought. Then he remembered the present that the old man had given him. He opened the little wooden box, hoping to find treasure, but inside was a tiny straw doll. He was very disappointed. "Doesn't the old man know that I hunt and fish? I don't play with dolls!"

Tirawa was about to close the lid, when he heard a tiny little voice. "I can give you your heart's desire!" it said. "Just ask!"

Tirawa was so surprised that he nearly dropped the box. It was beginning to get dark, so he thought he'd try out the straw doll's magic powers. "My heart's desire is to find a new tribe," Tirawa said.

The tiny little voice told him where he could find the tribe of Great Grey Otters. "They will make you very welcome," it said.

Although he was beginning to get tired, Tirawa kept going along the steep path until he came to a village. In the moonlight, he saw a circle of tepees and heard the sound of voices. The people of the village came out to meet Tirawa. Little Squirrel, the chief's beautiful daughter, brought him something to eat. "Welcome to our tribe," she said.

In the morning, the village chief called Tirawa into his tepee. He looked Tirawa up and down. "Where have you come from, young man? Can you hunt and fish?" asked the chief. Tirawa told him his story and the chief welcomed him to the tribe of the Great Grey Otters. Tirawa stayed in the village, hunting with the young men and talking with Little Squirrel whenever he could.

As they grew up, Tirawa and Little Squirrel fell deeply in love. One day, Tirawa asked the chief if he could marry her. The chief liked Tirawa very much, but he wanted Little Squirrel to marry a man from her own tribe, so he set him an impossible task. He said, "You may marry Little Squirrel only if you move that mountain out of the path of the morning sun."

That night Tirawa brought the little straw doll out of its dusty wooden box. "Please move the mountain for me," he said.

"Just as you ask," said the enchanted doll.

Next morning, the chief of the Great Grey Otters woke with the sun in his eyes. He looked out of his tepee, scarcely able to believe what he saw. "Tirawa has moved the mountain!" he said.

The chief decided to set Tirawa another task. He said, "I promise you can marry Little Squirrel, if you go across the lake and win the battle with that warring tribe on the other side." Everyone knew it was impossible. The tribe was the fiercest in the land. So Tirawa went off quietly to ask the little straw doll for help. Afterwards, he got into his canoe and paddled away.

All day the sound of fighting echoed across the lake. As night fell, the warring tribe ran away. Little Squirrel was feeling very sad. She didn't think she would ever see Tirawa again. "You must marry a man from the Great Grey Otters," her father said. A great wedding feast was prepared.

Tirawa was exhausted. He got back just as the guests were sitting down to a great wedding feast. "Please will you marry me?" he asked Little Squirrel. She was thrilled to see Tirawa, alive and well.

"I will," she said.

The chief wasn't very pleased, but he kept his promise. Tirawa and Little Squirrel were very happy together, so happy that they never again had to open the little wooden box and ask the enchanted doll for help.

The Enchanted Doll

Speaking and Listening

- *The Enchanted Doll* is based on a Native American folktale. Listen to the story, read aloud or take a copy and read it silently.

- Talk about how Native Americans were the original inhabitants of the North American continent and how they were skilled hunters and had distinct cultures of their own, believing in the spirits of the natural world (sun, moon, sky, river and tree spirits). Discuss how they lived in tribal groups and moved from place to place, following the movements of the animals they hunted.

- Tirawa excelled in a number of skills that were important to people who had to hunt for their food. List Tirawa's skills and discuss why they were necessary for a young Native American. Compare this with the things that people of our century need to learn, such as reading, IT and mathematics.

Tepees

- When the folktale was first told, long ago, Native Americans lived in tepees. Why would a tepee be important to people who followed the movements of the animals? Apart from a tent, what other kind of mobile homes can you think of?

The Straw Doll

- Imagine how Tirawa felt when he opened the lid of the wooden box and found, not gold or jewels, but a straw doll! Talk about occasions when you have experienced disappointment similar to Tirawa.

- Do you remember what the enchanted doll promised? Discuss what is meant by 'your heart's desire'.

- The enchanted doll was made of straw. In many countries it is customary to make corn dollies (of corn wheat and straw) to celebrate a successful harvest. Sometimes they used to be carried about as a magic token. Can you find out about any other harvest traditions?

Genie of the Lamp

- Talk about other folktales in which a creature or an object is given magical powers. Think of the Genie of the Lamp in *Aladdin* and the magic mirror in *Snow White*. Can you think of any more?

Language Activities

Bully Talk

- Tirawa's brothers were bullies. They were cruel and called him names. Discuss the problems of bullying and consider ways in which bullies can be helped to change their behaviour. Following your discussion on bullying, write down a list of ideas that might help bullies to change their ways, for example:

1. Share with a friend.
2. Walk to school with a friend.
3. Help my friend with work.
4. Play with a child who looks lonely.

Tirawa's Home

- Think about the place where Tirawa lived. Imagine the pine forest, the wide river and the high mountains. Talk about what more he might see (birds, the sky, small animals). Think about sounds (water splashing, trees creaking, owls hooting). Imagine sensations such as the feel of the sun on his back and the wind through his hair. Write a poem which explores Tirawa's home through the senses, making three-line verses from a list of sights, sounds and feelings. Then finish it off in your own way. For example:

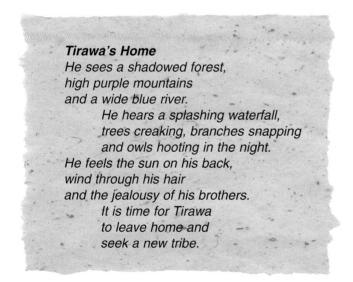

Tirawa's Home
He sees a shadowed forest,
high purple mountains
and a wide blue river.
    He hears a splashing waterfall,
    trees creaking, branches snapping
    and owls hooting in the night.
He feels the sun on his back,
wind through his hair
and the jealousy of his brothers.
    It is time for Tirawa
    to leave home and
    seek a new tribe.

Moving a Mountain

- Imagine how the chief of the Great Grey Otters must have felt when he said 'Tirawa has moved the mountain!' Work collaboratively to plan interviews with the chief, his daughter Little Squirrel, Tirawa and people of the tribe to find out what happened. Work out the questions that the interviewer should ask and provide answers in role as each character. Write down and record the interview dialogue with different characters taking part.

Disappointment

- Tirawa was very disappointed when he found the straw doll in the box. Have you ever had a disappointing present for your birthday or for Christmas? Write a short story about getting a disappointing present.

What's in the Box?

- Write a poem about opening a box, not knowing what's inside. First write about what it can't possibly be, because the box is too small, too light or not the right shape. Finish by saying what is in the box.

What's in the box?
It's not a football rolling about.
It's not an elephant trumpeting.
It's not a kite flying in the wind.
 But it might be
A baby doll dreaming dreams,
A fluffy kitten purring for milk,
A wind-up robot staring at me.
 Let's untie the ribbon,
 Tear off the paper
 And look inside the box!

- Fold a sheet of thin card to make a box-shape. Write your poem inside and fold down the top to make a lid. Use felt-tipped pens to make a bright design, such as birthday wrapping paper, on the lid.

Tirawa's Letter Home

- Tirawa's mother and father must have been very worried, wondering what might have happened to their youngest son. Write a reassuring letter from Tirawa to his parents, describing his adventures and telling them about the people who made him welcome.

Art Activities

Corn Dolly

- Make corn dolllies using pipe cleaners, straw, corn or raffia. Bind the pipe cleaners or raffia near the top in a contrasting colour, and spike up the ends to suggest hair. Add further binding to make a neck and then separate the pipe cleaners or raffia either side to make arms and hands. Make the body by adding binding for a waist, then divide the remaining pipe cleaners or raffia evenly to make legs. Twist the ends to create feet. Finally draw or stick on a face.

The Treasure Box

- Design a treasure box for Tirawa. Cover a shoe box with dry leaves, bits of sticks and moss, shells and small pebbles. Use strong glue to fix them in place. Coat the box with clear varnish or PVA glue. Line the box with scraps of silk or velvet and collect 'treasure' items, such as broken necklaces, to hide inside. Create a display table with a forest backdrop. Include branches, stones, pine cones and so on and, in the centre, place the open treasure box with 'jewels' spilling out.

Tirawa's Journey

- Take a roll of display paper and paint on the mountain scene from the story. Make the display long enough to go right along the wall. Paint purple mountains 'reaching for the sky', a deep pine forest and a blue river winding all the way to the village of the Great Grey Otters. Add animals, the hunter brothers, Tirawa and the old man. Paint and cut out decorated tepees for the chief's village and place the chief, his daughter and members of the tribe in the foreground. Edge the display with Native American-style designs.

Postcard Home

- Tirawa couldn't send a postcard, but he might have painted a picture of his new hunting ground to send to his parents. Paint the picture on an animal hide backing made by pasting several layers of newspaper together with flour paste. Add a layer of white kitchen paper on top. Make a simple wooden frame for the picture by overlapping four sticks at the corners and tying them with string. Attach to the backing.

Issunboshi's Sword

Once long ago, in Japan, there lived an old man and his wife. They were very happy together most of the time. But sometimes, when they heard children's voices echoing from the riverbank, the woman sighed. She longed for a child of her own. "I wish we had a tiny child," she said to her husband. "I'd love him even if he was no bigger than my little finger." And she sighed again.

One day, her wish came true and they had a baby boy. He was very small indeed, and no bigger than his mother's little finger. She called him Issunboshi which means 'Tiny One'. His mother fussed over him every minute of the day. She gave him lots of good things to eat, but Issunboshi didn't grow like other children. He grew up to be a very small man, no bigger than his father's first finger.

Issunboshi grew tired of his mother watching over him all the time, so he decided to leave home to visit the emperor and see the world. Before he left, Issunboshi asked his parents for a needle, a rice bowl and a pair of chopsticks. "I'll use the needle as a sword, the rice bowl as a boat and the chopsticks as oars to row with," he said. Although his parents thought this very strange, they gave him all he asked for and sadly waved goodbye. "Good luck!" they called, as they watched Issunboshi set off across the fields carrying the rice bowl on his head like a hat.

Issunboshi was so small that the grass and flowers towered over him like trees and the worms looked like pythons. He hadn't gone far when he met an ant. The ant looked as big as a horse to little Issunboshi. "Good morning, Ant," he said. "Can you please tell me how to get to the emperor's palace?" The ant told him the way. She said, "Go past the dandelions, walk across the field of horsetails and you'll reach the river. Sail down the river for a mile or two and you'll see the emperor's palace shining in the sun."

Issunboshi thanked the ant and went on his way, past the dandelions and through the field of horsetails until he came to the river. Then he climbed into his rice bowl boat and sailed off downstream, rowing as hard as he could with his chopstick oars.

Suddenly, a great golden fish swam up. "You look good enough to eat, little man," it said. It opened wide its big red mouth and showed all its sharp white teeth. Issunboshi was frightened, but he hit the fish on the head with his chopstick oars and it swam away down the river.

At last, after sailing all day long, Issunboshi came to the emperor's palace. It sparkled in the evening sun. Issunboshi was so small that he managed to creep in under the door and hide in a dark corner of the throne room where nobody could see him. When the emperor entered the room, Issunboshi knew he must be very brave. He climbed on to the emperor's knee, reached up and tugged at his pointed beard. "Your Exellency," he said, in his tiny tinny voice, "I have sailed in a rice bowl boat all the way down the river because I wanted so very much to meet you."

The emperor looked down at him. "Why are you so small?" he asked.

Issunboshi told the emperor about his mother and father and how they had wished for a tiny child, no bigger than his mother's little finger. The emperor liked the look of little Issunboshi, so he offered him a job at the palace. "You can teach my daughter to read," he said. The emperor's daughter was very beautiful and Issunboshi was delighted to teach her to read.

Every morning, Issunboshi helped the princess with her reading and every afternoon they walked in the palace gardens. One afternoon, an ugly ogre appeared on the path. He laughed aloud at the beautiful princess and the tiny man walking side by side and tried to push them aside.

"Don't go near the princess or you'll be sorry!" Issunboshi shouted in his tiny tinny voice.

This made the ogre laugh even louder. "What can you do to stop me, little man?" he said. He picked up Issunboshi and held him, between his thumb and forefinger, like a salted nut. Then he popped Issunboshi into his big red mouth and swallowed him whole. "Lovely grub!" he said, rubbing his great fat belly.

Then he let out a yowl of pain. "Ow, ow, ow!" wailed the ogre. He spat the little man out and ran away holding his stomach. Issunboshi had stabbed the ogre's insides with his sharp needle sword. "My hero!" said the beautiful princess. "You have saved my life, with your needle sword, Issunboshi!"

Issunboshi saw that the ogre had dropped something on the path in his rush to get away. It was a rattle decorated with bells. "What's this?" Issunboshi asked.

"We are very lucky," said the princess. "This is a magic rattle. If you shake it and make a wish, then your wish will come true." So Issunboshi shook the magic rattle until the bells rang loud and long. "I wish I could be the size of other men!" he said in his tiny tinny voice. In a moment, Issunboshi's wish came true and he grew taller and taller until he was taller than the princess.

"Will you marry me?" he asked the princess in his new deep voice.

The princess stood on tiptoe to kiss him. "Yes, please," she said.

When they went back to the palace, the emperor was surprised to meet the new tall Issunboshi and delighted to agree to his daughter's marriage. On the day of the wedding, everyone in the kingdom rejoiced. And Issunboshi and the princess lived happily together ever after.

Issunboshi's Sword

Speaking and Listening

- Listen to the tale *Issunboshi's Sword* read aloud. Can you think of other stories with finger- or thumb-sized characters? (*Thumbelina*, *Tom Thumb*, *Gulliver's Travels* and *Mrs Pepperpot*).

- Talk about how these tiny characters cope with the problems of living in a 'normal-sized' world. Imagine what you might use for a bed (a matchbox?), an umbrella (a waterlily leaf?), a stool (a mushroom?), a rocking chair (a walnut shell?) and so on.

- Discuss how Issunboshi set sail to the emperor's palace using a rice bowl as a boat and chopsticks as oars. Think of other vessels Issunboshi might have used to sail in.

- Demonstrate how chopsticks are used. Have a go at picking up food such as cornflakes or bits of apple using chopsticks.

Japan

- *Issunboshi's Sword* is a traditional tale from Japan, a mountainous country off the east coast of Asia which is made up of four main islands and several smaller ones. Can you find Japan on a world map or a globe?

- Make a collection of traditional Japanese artefacts (examples: rice bowl, chopsticks, Japanese kimono, pottery vase with a single stylish flower, a book on origami).

Ogres, Giants and Monsters

- The story tells us that an ugly ogre stopped Issunboshi and the princess on the path. Discuss what an ogre might look like and talk about the role of the ogre, monster or giant in a traditional folktale. They are usually included to show how the hero of the story manages to overcome difficulties in a blaze of glory.

Language Activities

Thesaurus

- The story tells us that Issunboshi was 'a tiny child', no bigger than his mother's little finger. Make a list of words that mean 'tiny', for example, small, little, minute and miniature.

- Think of comparisons or similes for small, for example, 'as small as a thimble', 'the height of a daisy', or 'the size of a pepperpot'. Write out your four best ideas.

Baby Issunboshi

- Use your comparisons to write a poem describing how Issunboshi looked when he was born, for example:

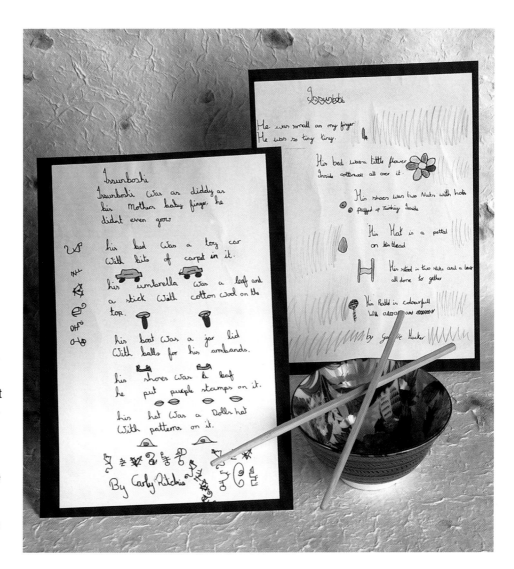

No bigger than his mother's finger,
as small as a bumble bee, Issunboshi
slept inside a buttercup, rocking
to the tune of a summer breeze.

or, to make it rhyme,

Issunboshi was a tiny child,
the size of a bumble bee,
just the height of a daisy
and almost too small to see.

What Happened Next?

- Consider what might happen after the story ends. Imagine a scene in which Issunboshi and his bride go back to visit his father and mother in their cottage by the riverbank. Will they recognise their tall handsome son? Work in groups to make up a short conversation between mother, father, Issunboshi and the princess.

- Develop the scene and record it as a play script. Consider the changes in Issunboshi, for example, his height, deep voice and expensive clothes. Think about his parents' introduction as a poor elderly couple to their new daughter-in-law, the princess. How will they feel about it? This can be an impromptu dramatisation or a formal short play.

I Wish ...

- The story tells us that the ogre dropped a magic rattle in his rush to escape Issunboshi's needle sword. What wish would you make if you found the magic rattle?

Japanese Haiku

- A haiku is a Japanese poem written in a special pattern. It is made up of three lines. The first line has five syllables (or beats), the second has seven and the last line has five. Practise counting syllables by thinking of one-beat, two-beat, three-beat names and so on. 'Tom' is a one-syllable name and 'Reiko' is two. How many syllables are in 'Issunboshi'?

Magic Haiku

- Think of words that Issunboshi might have said when shaking the magic rattle. Write a magic spell for Issunboshi, following the haiku form.

- Write your haiku on a decorated rice bowl shape.

Mini-books

- Issunboshi was so small that he must have learned to read from very tiny books. Make a mini-diary or a miniature story book suitable for Issunboshi to use. Information about Japanese traditions or the story of Issunboshi could be recorded in it.

Issunboshi's Adventures

- The story tells us that Issunboshi had many adventures before he reached the emperor's palace. Issunboshi first met an ant who showed him the way to the river, telling him to go by the dandelions and through a field of horsetails ... . There, a fierce golden fish tried to eat him up. Remembering how small Issunboshi was, invent more adventures that he may have had. Perhaps he met a grasshopper who looked as huge as a dinosaur or a hungry bird or a worm that looked as big as a snake? Make it into one long wall story.

Invitation to a Wedding

- Look at wedding invitations, noting the special form of words, for example:

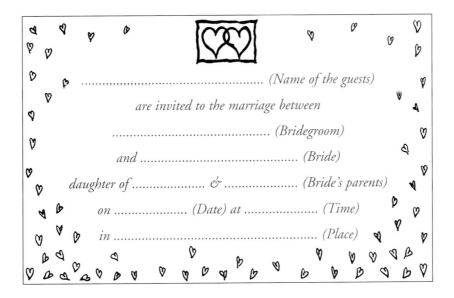

- Make up invitations to the wedding of Issunboshi to the princess, imagining where and when it will take place. Try to find Japanese names to suit the characters and decorate the edges of the invitations with a flower pattern in felt-tipped pen.

Art Activities

WANTED!

- Paint a picture of the 'ugly ogre' from the story. We don't know a lot about him, except that he has 'a great fat belly'. Make the ogre look very fierce, perhaps brandishing a cruel wooden club. Imagine that the ogre has a price on his head and make your picture into a WANTED! poster.

River Print

- Hokusai was a famous Japanese artist who lived over 200 years ago. He created beautiful woodcut prints of mountains and rivers. Make a print of a scene from the story by scratching your picture on a polystyrene art tile. Coat the tile with printing ink and carefully press it down on a piece of paper. Rub a soft cloth across the back of the paper, then gently ease the paper away. Leave your print to dry.

The Emperor's Palace

- Look at pictures of fairy-tale palaces and castles to give you ideas for designing the emperor's palace. The story tells us only that the emperor's palace sparkled in the sun. Paint purple mountains and a high yellow sun on a deep blue background. When it is dry, use white paper with gold towers and black windows to create the palace. In the foreground, add the river using either paint or cut Cellophane and foil so that the river sparkles in the sun.

Boat Race

- Origami is the Japanese art of paper-folding. It is a skill which has been passed down through the generations. Make a simple origami boat, following the instructions provided. Decorate your boat and test the boats by floating them across the water tank or a playground puddle.

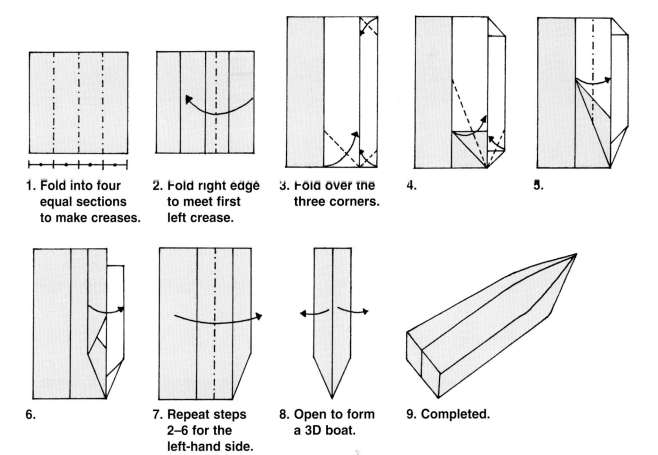

1. Fold into four equal sections to make creases.

2. Fold right edge to meet first left crease.

3. Fold over the three corners.

4.

5.

6.

7. Repeat steps 2–6 for the left-hand side.

8. Open to form a 3D boat.

9. Completed.

The King's Sandals

Once upon a time, there lived a king who hated getting wet. He didn't like going out in the rain. He didn't like paddling in the sea, and he simply hated having a bath.

The king hadn't washed for such a long time that he began to smell. Royal servants held their noses as they passed him and the queen said, "If you don't have a bath soon, I'm going to live by myself at the other side of the palace."

The king was very fond of the queen and didn't want to be left on his own. He would feel very lonely during the nights and would be frightened by the dark shadows beside his bed, so he decided that bath-time could not be put off any longer.

Next morning the king said, "Today I am going to have a bath," and he marched down towards the river. The servants were very excited. They scurried after him with soap and fluffy white towels. Everyone wanted to see the king having his first bath for years.

There was a buzz of excitement in the town, too, as the townspeople said to one another, "Guess what? The king is going to have a bath!" They could hardly believe their ears, so they all ran down to the river to watch. When the king and queen arrived, everyone fell silent. As the king stood shivering on the bank, people stood on tiptoe to get a better view.

The king paddled into the river. "It's cold – and the water is wet!" he shouted. "I don't like it!" But he ordered the servants to bring him a large cake of best-scented soap and he scrubbed himself all over until the river was bubbling with foam. "Is that better?" he asked, beginning to enjoy himself.

"Now wash your hair!" called the queen. So the king ordered the servants to bring him a bottle of shampoo and did as he was told.

When he was quite clean, he climbed out onto the riverbank and Wafi, his favourite servant, brought him a white fluffy towel. When he had finished drying himself, the king saw that his feet were dusty. "Bother!" he said. "I must have forgotten to wash my feet."

He paddled back into the river and scrubbed his feet as hard as he could, but when he climbed out, they were still dusty. So he tried again, and again. Every time the king put his feet on the ground, they got dusty once more. "That's it! The earth must be dirty!" he said.

The king called for Wafi. "Wafi," he said, "the earth is dirty. Clean it up at once!"

"Yes certainly, your majesty. Immediately, your majesty," Wafi said, wondering how he could possibly do such a thing. Then he had a brilliant idea. He called for the servants to bring dustpans and brushes and commanded them to sweep the earth clean for the king. This raised

a great cloud of dust. Everyone, including the king, soon began to cough and choke.

"Enough! Enough!" said the king. "Wafi, think of something else."

"What can I do this time?" Wafi wondered to himself. Then he had another good idea. This time he decided to wash the earth, so he asked the other servants to bring scrubbing brushes and buckets of hot water. He even asked the townspeople to help. Soon a great army of people were sloshing hot water all over the earth. Then they got down on their knees and began to scrub the earth. They made everything so wet and soapy that the land turned into a giant mud bath.

"This is useless, Wafi," grumbled the king. "I'll get my feet muddy next time I have a bath. You'll have to think again."

"Yes, certainly, your majesty," said Wafi, all the while thinking to himself that he might never have another good idea in his whole life! He twiddled his pencil and scratched his head, but he couldn't think of a thing. "I'll have to sleep on it," he thought and went off to bed.

Next morning, Wafi jumped out of bed, shouting, "I've got the best idea ever! I'll cover the earth with a carpet. That should keep everything clean and dry for the royal feet!" So he ordered everyone in the land to bring a piece of leather, a needle and cotton. They all got down on their knees and together they began to stitch a huge patchwork quilt of all different patterns and colours. The people worked for seven days and seven nights. When the bright leather quilt was finished, it was laid carefully over the earth.

The king was delighted. When next he went down to the river for a bath, he stepped out onto the leather quilt and his feet were spotlessly clean and dry. "Bravo, Wafi!" he cried. "What a splendid idea!" Then he thanked all the townspeople for helping.

The king's gardener was the only sad person in the vast crowd of people. He walked across the leather quilt and said to the king, "What about the grass, your majesty? What about the queen's flowers? You know how much she loves her flowers. They can't grow if there is a leather quilt over everything."

The king looked worried. "Indeed, indeed," he said. "What shall I do?"

The gardener took a pair of secateurs from his apron. He knelt down and carefully cut the leather quilt around the king's feet. Then he took two laces from his pocket and tied the leather to the soles of his feet.

The king was wearing the very first pair of sandals in the world. He tried walking. He tried jumping. He tried running. Now he was able to have a bath every morning, and whenever he stepped out of the water, he put on his leather sandals. They kept his feet bone-dry and perfectly clean.

The King's Sandals

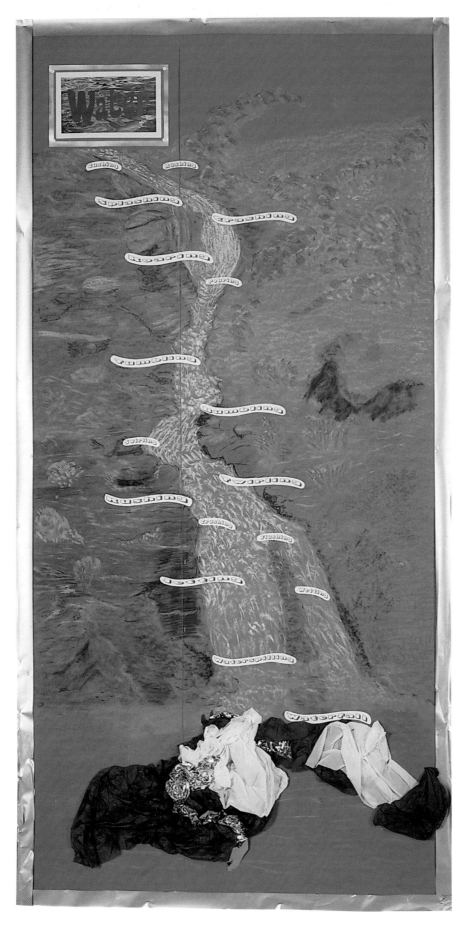

Speaking and Listening

- Listen to *The King's Sandals* read aloud or take a copy of the story and read silently. Discuss the king's dislike of water and think about all the good things he is missing.

- Think about how important it is to be clean and how cleanliness keeps us healthy.

- Wafi and the king thought of three different ways of keeping the king's feet clean. Can you think of any more?

India

- The story is set in India. Can you find the Republic of India on a map of the world?

Water

- Explore the sensation of water and find words to describe how it feels and moves, for example, wet, watery, cool, runny, drips, drops, spills, squirts. Make a wall dictionary of water words.

Sandals

- Think about the way the gardener made sandals for the king. Gather a variety of sandals to display and compare them with the king's first pair. What materials are sandals made of?

Making Plants Grow

- Consider why the queen's flowers would die if a leather quilt covered them. Talk about what plants and flowers need to make them grow.

Language Activities

Sandals for Sale

- When the gardener invented a pair of leather sandals for the king, they were the first in the world. Imagine that you had invented the first pair of sandals. How would you try and sell them? How would you advertise them? Design an advert to bring sandals to the notice of everybody in India. It should exaggerate all the good points and encourage people to buy, for example:

- Perhaps add a phrase to say that the sandals will keep your feet clean after your bath – just like the king! Print your advert in bold colours and illustrate with a picture of the king's sandals.

Through New Eyes

- We hear a lot about the king in this story, but very little about the queen or anyone else. Rewrite the story so that it is told in the first person, as if you are the king, which means using 'I' and 'me' throughout.

- Explore what is happening through the eyes of another character in the story. Imagine you are Wafi, the king's servant, the queen, the gardener or even the king himself.

BY ROYAL APPOINTMENT

SANDAL-MAKER
TO HIS MAJESTY

BE THE FIRST
TO WEAR THE LATEST
ALL-LEATHER STYLE

Royal Instructions

- We know that the king called on Wafi to tell the servants to clean up the earth for him. Perhaps he put a notice on the wall of the servants' quarters similar to the one shown.

- Write out a similar set of instructions for other ways of cleaning up the earth for the king. Remember to keep your instructions clear and concise.

To all royal servants

1. Assemble on the riverbank at 8am.
2. Bring brushes and a dustpan.
3. Sweep the earth clean for His Majesty.
4. Wait for your work to be inspected.
5. Stand down and return to your quarters.

Water

- List all the things water is good for (washing, drinking, making tea and so on). Then make another list of games you like to play in water, such as paddling, splashing and making mud pies. Use some of the ideas to make a list poem, beginning each verse with a different person's ideas about water.

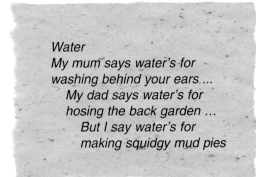

*Water
My mum says water's for
washing behind your ears ...
My dad says water's for
hosing the back garden ...
But I say water's for
making squidgy mud pies*

- You could add *My grandma says ... My auntie says ...* and to link it with the story *The king says ... .*

- Write your finished poem inside a zigzag book and illustrate each verse.

Keeping Healthy

- Make a list of the things we need to keep clean, including soap and water, a shower or bath, towels, toothbrush, toothpaste.

- Write a report about the importance of washing hair, brushing teeth, showering or bathing and wearing clean clothes.

- Write about how important water is for drinking and helping us to keep healthy. Make this a factual piece of work. Use the reports to compile a book about keeping clean and healthy.

Simple Indian Cookery

- Find a recipe for a traditional Indian dish and write out the instructions so that someone else can follow them. First you must compile a list of ingredients, then a method to tell your reader what to do.

Art Activities

The Leather Quilt

- Make a display panel, showing the deep blue river and a patchwork leather quilt covering the land. Each child can contribute a different patterned square using stripes, squiggles, spots and so on. Join the quilt using black felt-tipped pens to indicate the stitches. Turn back one section to show the green grass beneath. Add a cut-out of the king contemplating the cold blue water and show the palace in the distance. Edge the display with a repeated pattern of Indian elephants.

- Make a quilt by cutting scraps of material into equal squares. Join into one large quilt by sewing the squares together with thick cotton. Bind the edges of the quilt to prevent fraying. Iron and pin to the wall.

Sandals fit for a King

- Cut out pictures of different sandals from catalogues and magazines. Make a sandal collage, overlapping the pictures. Display alongside a variety of sandals on a seascape background. Arrange the sandals on sand and add pebbles and shells.

- Make sandals fit for a king by cutting narrow strips, like laces, from felt or material that looks like leather. Make the soles of the sandals by drawing round a child's feet on paper for the template. Cut the shapes out of felt. Sew the strips to the sole-shapes and tie up the sandals, just as the king's gardener did.

Indian Spices

- Bring in a variety of Indian spices. Look at the colour and texture of coriander, chilli powder, ginger, turmeric, cloves, cinnamon and so on. Smell a pinch of each spice. Make a spice mosaic by putting a little of each on sticky see-through plastic. Put the spices on a grid, naming each one.

Lord of the Winds

Far away, in the wild cold lands of the north, there lived a village chief with three daughters. One night a fierce storm blew up, much worse than any storm that had gone before. The bitter wind did not stop for three whole weeks. No one could hunt or fish, so the villagers grew weak and hungry. "If the wind doesn't die down soon, it will kill us all," said the chief to his daughters. "Kotura, Lord of the Winds, must be very angry with us. We must send him a wife to keep him happy." So the chief sent his eldest daughter to be Kotura's wife.

He told her that the pure white snowbird would fly down to perch on her shoulder. "Be kind to him," he said, "and he will help you." So the eldest daughter set off, trudging through the deep snow, keeping her face to the north.

When the snowbird fluttered down, the girl was so cold that she forgot what her father had said. She shouted at the bird and waved him away.

When at last she reached Kotura's tent, he was surprised to see the eldest daughter. "What are you doing here?" he asked in his loud booming voice. "My father sent me to be your wife," she told him. She was very tired, but the Lord of the Winds would not let her rest. "Cook some meat for my supper, girl," he ordered. "And give the rest to the snowbird."

The eldest daughter made Kotura's supper, but the blizzard still raged outside and she couldn't see where she was going, so she threw the snowbird's meat away and went back to Kotura with an empty plate.

"Did you do what I told you?" he asked. The girl nodded. "Then show me what the snowbird gave you in return." She showed him the empty plate. Kotura said nothing and just handed the eldest daughter a deerskin. "Make me a pair of mittens, girl," he ordered. The girl didn't know where to start. "Didn't the snowbird tell you what to do?" asked Kotura.

"No," said the eldest daughter.

"You didn't go near the snowbird!" shouted Kotura. "I don't want a disobedient girl like you for a wife!" And he threw the eldest daughter into a deep snowdrift where she froze to death.

Kotura was so angry he sent a truly terrible wind to the wild cold lands of the north. The village chief and his two daughters hid away. "The Lord of the Winds will destroy us," he said to them. "Your sister must have disobeyed him." So he sent his second daughter to be Kotura's wife. "Be kind to the snowbird," he told her.

The second daughter trudged through the deep snow, keeping her face to the north. When the snowbird perched on her shoulder, she too shouted at him and waved him away. When she got to Kotura's tent, the girl was exhausted, but she was not allowed to rest. Kotura told her to

48

make his supper and then give some to the snowbird. But the biting wind was so fierce that she too threw the snowbird's meat away and returned to Kotura with an empty plate.

"Did you do what I told you?" he asked. The girl nodded. After he had eaten, Kotura gave the second daughter a sealskin and ordered her to make him a pair of shoes, but she didn't know where to begin.

"Didn't the snowbird tell you what to do?" The second daughter shook her head. "I don't want a disobedient wife like you!" roared Kotura. And he threw her into the icy waters of the river.

Kotura was so enraged that he sent an even more savage storm to the wild cold lands of the north. The village chief and his youngest daughter hid away. "The Lord of the Winds will demolish us for good this time!" said the chief. "Your sister must have disobeyed him." So, sad at heart, he sent his youngest daughter to be Kotura's wife. She trudged through the deep snow, keeping her face to the north.

When the snowbird fluttered on to the young girl's shoulder, she stroked his tired wings and sheltered him under her cloak. He hopped down at the door of Kotura's tent as the girl crept inside.

Although she was extremely tired, the youngest daughter made Kotura's supper, then went out in the bitter wind to feed the snowbird. "How kind you are," said the gentle white bird. "Follow me." He led the girl to a tent, almost hidden beneath the snow. An old woman looked out. "Who are you?" she asked. "What brings you here?" The snowbird told the old woman how kind the girl had been and asked the old woman to reward her, so she gave the youngest daughter two sharp knives and some bone needles and told her how to make a coat for Kotura.

Afterwards, she trudged back through the snow to the Lord of the Winds. "Why were you so long?" he asked. The youngest daughter held out the plate and showed Kotura the needles and sharp knives that the old woman had given her. "You will be able to make me some fine clothes with these," he said.

After he had eaten, Kotura gave the youngest daughter a caribou skin and ordered her to make him a coat. She scraped and cut the skin as the old woman had taught her. Next, she sewed it into a coat. The coat fitted Kotura perfectly. He was delighted. "You have done well, youngest daughter," he said. "I'd like you to become my wife."

So the youngest daughter married the Lord of the Winds and immediately the sun shone on the wild cold lands of the north. The villagers rejoiced that they were able to hunt and fish again, just as before.

49

Lord of the Winds

Speaking and Listening

- Listen to the story *Lord of the Winds* being read aloud or take a copy and read it silently. *Lord of the Winds* is a folktale from Alaska, a frozen land 'on top of the world', where the coastline is ice-bound in winter and a cold arctic wind blows across its snow-covered mountains nearly all year round.

- Alaska is now the most northern part of the United States of America. It is divided from the US by Canada. Can you find it on a world map or globe?

- Alaska is a land of ice and snow, almost all year round. Such a cold climate makes it a difficult place to live. Use a variety of information sources to find out about Alaska.

- Talk about how, at the time of the story, the tribes of the Far North lived only by fishing and by hunting seal and caribou (reindeer), so when 'the bitter wind did not stop for three whole weeks,' the villagers had little to eat and soon went hungry.

Caribou

- In North America, reindeer are called 'caribou'. The name 'caribou' comes from an Indian word meaning 'snow shoveller'. Why do you think this is? Find out about caribou and consider the appropriateness of its name. (Caribou use their hooves like shovels to dig under the snow for food.)

The Snowbird

- The snowbird in the story was probably the Canadian snow goose. Find out about snow geese, using a variety of information sources.

Sad Endings

- *The Lord of the Winds*, like many other folktales, does not have a happy ending for everyone. Some stories show little sympathy for the characters who get in the way of the narrative. Discuss folktales where some of the characters are 'punished', sent away or even killed.

Language Activities

Snow Poem

- Think about the way snow falls from a winter sky and write down some movement words, for example, whirling, dancing, drifting, fluttering. Use your set of movement words to create images for a snow poem.

Snow
whirling
like feathers from a torn quilt,
dancing
like a ballerina on pointy feet.

- Display your snow poems firstly by writing them out on a sheet of paper. Cover the sheet completely with another of the same size, then hold both papers against a window and mark out the shape of the poem on the top sheet. Cut out the marked area and decorate around the frame with pastel crayons, then glue the frame over the poem.

On Top of the World

- Alaska is a frozen land, said to be 'on top of the world'. Write a poem describing what you would see if you were looking down from the 'top of the world'. Remember you are looking down on everything and everyone, so begin by making a list of things below you, for example, clouds, snowbirds and mountain tops. Make the scene sound very cold and white, for example:

On Top of the World
Far down below,
clouds fat with snow,
icy mountain tops,
white on white on white
like snowbirds flying
a winter sky.

A Caribou Journey

- Find out about the way the caribou live and write an account of the journey they take in huge herds. Think about how hard it must be to trek for hundreds of miles in bitter weather. Think about the daily hunt for food and how much caribou must enjoy the warmer summer weather. Put your account inside an eight-page booklet.

Letter Home

- Imagine you are the village chief's youngest daughter. Write a letter home to your father. Tell him about the wedding to Kotura, the snowbird and some of the tasks you have to tackle every day. Write your letter in the shape of a tepee. (See the photograph on page 2.)

And They Lived Happily Ever After

- Not everyone in *The Lord of the Winds* lives 'happily ever after'. Try rewriting the story, so that there is a happy ending for everyone. Work out ways in which the two eldest daughters might manage to escape from Kotura, for example, by kayak (canoe) or by sled or by riding on the wings of the snowbird. The escapes must suit the story's setting and fit in with the time and place of the original.

Art Activities

Snowflakes and Crystals

- Make 'snow crystal' designs from white paper. Take a hexagonal sheet of paper and fold it in half and half again to create six triangles. Cut out bite-size shapes from the triangles, so that no two patterns are exactly alike. Unfold and paste onto dark backing paper. Make a tabletop display of items associated with snow.

- Create snowflakes by cutting kitchen paper or blotting paper into circles. Draw a snowflake pattern on the paper with a water-based black or blue felt-tipped pen. Then spray a little water over the picture. As the paper becomes damp, the pattern becomes misty and spreads into rainbow colours. Paste onto a silver foil background.

Animal Hides

- The three daughters in the story were asked by Kotura to make mittens, slippers and a coat from animal hides. Design and make a pair of mittens or a pair of slippers for Kotura using felt. Embroider patterns on them as the women would have done.

Trekking Across the Snows

- Make a display showing snow-clad mountains in the background, the tops of a few conifers and miles of snow. Add a long trail of migrating caribou in silhoutte. Show the tracks their hooves have made across the snow. Use the background to display the children's poems. (See page 52.)

And the Sun Shone

- Paint pictures of Kotura and his bride and display them on a dramatic background showing the rising sun, spilling red, orange and yellow light over mountains and the Arctic Sea.

Maya's Winter Violets

Once there was a young girl called Maya who lived with her stepmother and her stepsister in a cottage deep in the forest. Maya's stepmother made her scrub and polish and clean all day long. Maya felt very tired and by bedtime she was exhausted. Her stepsister didn't like her very much. Sometimes, Maya felt very sad and lonely.

One winter's day, when a bitter wind was blowing through the trees by the cottage, Maya's stepsister said, "I need some fresh flowers for my bedroom. Maya, go into the forest and pick some violets for me."

"But I won't find any violets blooming in December!" said Maya.

"You heard what your sister said!" shouted her stepmother. "Go and pick a bunch of violets for her."

So Maya, who was wearing only a thin cotton dress, set off into the forest. It was very cold. The wind howled through the trees and snow lay deep on the ground. Maya shivered in her summer dress and thin shoes. She wrapped her arms around her body and tried to stop her teeth from chattering. She thought she might freeze to death. "What shall I do?" she wondered. "I dare not go home without some violets for my sister."

As Maya stumbled through the snow, she suddenly saw bright flames flickering amongst the trees. Flames meant a fire and a fire promised warmth. She hurried towards the flickering flames. There, sitting in a great circle around a huge bonfire, Maya saw twelve strange men wearing long cloaks. Each cloak was of different colours. One of the men, who seemed to be very old indeed, was dressed in a magnificent cloak of silver and white. He had white hair and a long white beard. He sat on a high chair like a throne and seemed to be in charge. "Come and warm yourself by the fire, my dear," he said. Maya stretched out her freezing hands to the flames.

"What brings you into the forest on a night like this?" asked the old man.

"My sister sent me out to pick a bunch of violets for her," she said. "I daren't go home until I find them."

"But this is the month of December," said the old man. "Violets don't bloom until March. You won't find any at this time of the year."

Maya began to cry. "Please, please, can you help me?" she pleaded.

The twelve men gathered closer together. They stroked their beards and whispered to one another. Then the one in silver and white, who seemed to be the oldest of them all, explained, "We are the Twelve Months of the Year, so it's lucky you bumped into us. I am the month of December, my child, so it is my turn to sit on the throne. But, of course, we'd like to help you. This is our plan. We will all move three places to the left."

The twelve men nodded and smiled at Maya. They all moved three chairs to the left and a young man wearing a green and yellow cloak climbed on to the throne. Maya wondered to herself how this was going to help her, but she didn't have long to wait to find out. "I am the month of March," said the young man.

Immediately, the snow melted and pale sunlight shone through the trees. Green leaves appeared on the branches and the ground was covered with bright yellow buttercups and sweet-smelling violets. Maya turned her cold face up to the sun. Then she knelt down and gathered great handfuls of violets into her apron. "Thank you, thank you, dear Months," she called, as she ran back home through the leafy forest.

As she neared the cottage, a bitter wind began to howl through the bare black trees and the snow once more lay deep on the ground. Maya stumbled through the snow and pushed open the cottage door. She tumbled the sweet-smelling violets on to the table. Her stepmother glared at her, "Where on earth did you get these flowers?" she asked.

Maya explained that she had met the Twelve Months of the Year in the depths of the forest. "Do you mean that you could have had anything you wanted?" her stepmother asked.

Maya nodded. "I thought you'd be pleased," she said.

"Pleased? Pleased?" By now her stepmother was shouting with rage. "What a stupid girl you are! Why bring a few violets when you could have had apples or grapes or strawberries? Think of the money we could make in the market selling fruit out of season!"

"Why don't we go and see the Twelve Months for ourselves, mother," said the stepsister. So they put on their warmest coats and fur boots and took a basket from the kitchen. "We'll make sure we get lots of expensive fruit to sell in the market," they said.

They trudged through the deep snow until they saw the light of a bonfire in the middle of the forest. Around it sat the Twelve Months, with the old man, December, on the throne.

"You gave my daughter violets," Maya's stepmother said. "We want apples and grapes and strawberries!"

"I didn't see your daughter," said December.

"It's no use talking to him," the stepsister said. She turned to young January. "Young man, give us some expensive fruit!"

Without a word, the Twelve Months changed places once more. This time January sat on the throne.

Immediately, an even more bitter wind began to blow and icicles hung from the trees. The stepmother and her daughter shrivelled up in the frosty air and the bitter wind blew them like dry leaves, high over the treetops. They never returned to the little cottage in the forest. Maya didn't miss them. She lived happily by herself, tending her lovely garden where, to everyone's surprise, flowers and fruit and vegetables grew all year round.

Maya's Winter Violets

Speaking and Listening

- Listen to *Maya's Winter Violets* read aloud. The story is based on a Bohemian folktale. Bohemia is now part of the Czech Republic. Can you find the Czech Republic on a map of the world?

Months of the Year

- Go over the sequence of the months of the year. Talk about the 'twelve strange men wearing long cloaks' that Maya met. Why do you think the oldest (December) was dressed in silver and white? Discuss appropriate colours for the other Months of the Year to be dressed in.

Traditional Story Conventions

- Maya lived with her stepmother and stepsister who were very unkind to her. Can you think of other traditional stories where there are horrid step families?

Language Activities

Months of the Year

- Look for poems which follow the sequence of the months, for example:

Calendar of Clothes
January is a time for coats,
for caps and fur-lined boots.
February likes hats with flaps and
zipped-up coloured ski-suits.

From *Calendar of Clothes*, first published
by OUP

- Discuss ideas for a new 'around the year' poem, thinking about the weather, fruit and flowers that each month might bring and the clothes suitable for wearing each month.

Letter to the Months

- Write a letter to your favourite month of the year. Follow the usual conventions of letter writing and say what you like best about your chosen month. Refer to the weather, flowers that bloom or things that you like to do or look forward to during that month. Add illustrations which reflect the month to whom you are writing.

An Impossible Task

- Discuss the impossibility of finding violets growing in the month of December and think about other equally difficult tasks. Rewrite Maya's story making the main character a boy, urged by his stepfather and stepbrother to bring back something quite impossible, for example, next week's newspaper. Set your story in the city streets.

Poems from Packets

- Write a 'found poem' using some of the words from the back of a seed packet, for example:

  'A very special violet; the delicate blooms change from pale blue through to sea blue then a rich purple. These violets will provide valuable spring colour from March to early summer.'

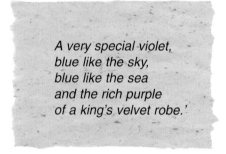

*A very special violet,
blue like the sky,
blue like the sea
and the rich purple
of a king's velvet robe.'*

- Illustrate with a picture of violets in bloom and edge with a green and purple border.

Purple Poem

- Consult a thesaurus to find as many names for the colour purple as possible. List the names, such as mulberry, lavender and heliotrope, and use them to create a poem, exploring the sounds of the words and concentrating on alliteration. Display your purple poem on a page lightly crayoned or washed over in shades of violet.

Flowers of Winter

- Maya is sent to look for violets in December. Use information sources to find flowers that could be picked in December, for example, Christmas roses, aconites and winter jasmine. Make a booklet to record your findings and illustrate.

Violets

- Find out about violets. When in the year do they bloom? What is their flower-colour and leaf-shape? Where do they grow? Where did Maya find her violets? What part of the story tells you that violets have a lovely perfume?

- The violet used to be called 'heartsease', a sixteenth-century name which means that it is supposed to make you feel at peace with the world. Can you invent another name for the violet? (Examples: heartspeace, sweetheart flower, happyheart, purplekiss.)

58

Art Activities

Months of the Year

- Design an appropriate headdress for each of the Twelve Months of the Year. For example, December might wear a crown of bare branches or holly, September a headdress decorated with ripe apples and pears, and August a crown of bright golden sunflowers. What might April or October wear?

Bonfire in the Forest

- Make a large collaborative collage of the bonfire scene from the story and arrange the Twelve Months of the Year in order around the bonfire.

The Colour Purple

- Show the children how red and blue can be mixed to make purple. Encourage them to experiment, adding white where necessary. Make a colour ladder showing the range of purple colours, from the palest lavender to the deepest purple.

- Using all the violet shades you have made, paint pictures to illustrate the description of 'the ground covered with sweet-smelling violets.'

Flowers around the Year

- Make a wheel, divided into twelve segments, showing flowers likely to be in flower at each month of the year. Draw and colour examples or cut out illustrations from seed packets or garden catalogues.

Maya's Lovely Garden

- The story ends by describing Maya's lovely garden where 'flowers and fruit and vegetables grew all year round.' Design Maya's garden and include trees heavy with fruit, rows of vegetables and a riot of flowers. Make the sun shine and have bright butterflies and insects flying free across the garden. Perhaps show Maya happily watering her flowers.

Tian and the Cranes

Long ago, in the land of China, there was an old man called Tian who lived on top of a high mountain, so high that it nearly touched the sky. Although he lived alone, the old man was never lonely. He had lots of friends among the cranes, great wide-winged birds that flew down from the clouds to visit him every day. Tian fed them and cared for them.

One day, Tian left his lonely mountain home to visit the busy city. He wanted to find out if the people were still being kind and generous to each other. He wrapped a fine embroidered cloak around his thin shoulders. The fastest and strongest crane stooped down and Tian climbed between the bird's wide white wings. It took him to the city in the valley below.

Soon Tian began to miss the silence of the high mountains and to long for his lonely home. The city was full of noise and bustle. Tian walked along the crowded streets until he met a beggar. He asked the beggar if he would be willing to exchange his ragged clothes for his own embroidered cloak. "Your cloak is much too fine for a poor man like me," protested the beggar.

Tian told him that he had come to test the people of the city and that nobody should guess who he was. When the beggar understood that Tian was a very special person, he agreed to change clothes with him. Tian thanked the beggar and went on his way.

Every morning, Tian sat in the streets with a begging bowl at his feet. Rich people passed him by, taking no notice of the old man. They didn't stop to put money in his bowl. Tian felt very disappointed in the people of the city and he grew very hungry indeed.

One evening, he knocked on the door of an inn. When Mr Wang, the innkeeper, came out, Tian asked if he could please give him something to eat. Then he added, "I'm sorry, but I have no money to pay for it." "Don't worry," said the innkeeper. "You look in need of a good meal." Tian sat down and Mr Wang brought him some rice, a bowl of rich soup and a cup of green tea. Then, he settled the old man in a bed for the night.

From that time on, Tian spent his days on the streets of the city and came back to the inn each evening. Every night, the innkeeper gave the old man a cup of green tea, a hot meal and a bed to sleep in. "You're always welcome here," Mr Wang told him.

After many months, Tian said to the innkeeper. "You have been very good to me. I'd like to find a way to repay you." "Nonsense," replied the innkeeper. "I'm only too pleased to be able to help a poor old man like you."

Tian said, "I have no money, but I'll give you something very special instead." With that, he took a fine paintbrush from the bundle he carried on his back and began to paint a beautiful picture of three cranes on the wall of the inn. The innkeeper could scarcely believe his eyes. "Wonderful!" he breathed.

Tian started to sing and clap his hands and one by one the three cranes fluttered off the wall and began to dance. It was a slow graceful dance, their elegant legs keeping time to Tian's music. "Please tell me who you are," called Mr Wang. But Tian had disappeared.

Soon Mr Wang's inn became very famous. It was crowded night after night. Everyone was talking about the wonderful dancing cranes. Lots of people came to see them and to buy food and drink at the inn. Mr Wang became one of the richest men in the city. But he always had a spare bed and hot meal to give to any poor beggar who stopped to knock at his door.

It was many months before Tian went back to the inn. The innkeeper was delighted to see him again. As usual, he brought the old man some rice, a bowl of rich soup and a cup of green tea. "Please tell me who you are, good sir," he said, but Tian just shook his head and smiled.

When he had finished his meal, Tian took a flute from his bundle and began to play a haunting tune. "It's like music from heaven," sighed the innkeeper. "I"m a lucky man to have heard it."

Slowly, the three cranes folded their great white wings and stepped down from the wall. They knelt in front of the old man who climbed on to the back of the biggest and strongest, saying to the innkeeper, "Always remember to look after others as you have looked after me. Good-bye, my friend."

Tian raised his flute to his lips and played one last tune. The innkeeper watched sadly as a great flock of cranes appeared and surrounded him and they all flew off into the evening sky. Mr Wang stood in his doorway watching them long after the sun had set.

The cranes took Tian back to his lonely home on the mountain top. The innkeeper never saw him again, but he always had a hot meal and a bed ready just in case Tian should ever return. From that day on Mr Wang was always kind and generous to any poor beggar who came knocking on his door.

Tian and the Cranes

Speaking and Listening

- Listen to the story of *Tian and the Cranes* read aloud. *Tian and the Cranes* is a version of an ancient Chinese story, one which was handed down as part of a 'storytelling' script or haupen. Classic stories became as well known in China through opera, as they did in book form. The tradition of re-telling Chinese stories by acting, miming and singing is more than a thousand years old.

- Discuss where Tian lived ('on top of a high mountain'). What would his home look like? In Chinese, 'Tian' means 'Heaven'. Why do you think Tian was given this name?

- Tian lived alone, but was never lonely. Explore this idea. Tian had some unusual friends. Think about having no one to talk to, only birds. Can you think of other people who may only have animals to keep them company?

- Discuss the reasons for Tian's visit to the city and talk about the people he met there. Consider aspects of Tian's life that show he was no ordinary person.

- Imagine the excitement of riding between a 'bird's wide white wings'. What might you see around and below you?

China

- China is a huge country with some very high mountains. Those in Tibet are so high that they are known as 'the roof of the world'. Do you think that this is where Tian might have lived? Find Tibet on a map of the world and try to locate some of the mountains.

Cranes

- The story tells us that Tian made friends with the cranes and fed and cared for them. Cranes are very graceful birds with long powerful beaks and long necks and legs. They are the world's tallest birds, standing about two metres high. They fly with their necks extended and their legs stretched out behind. Think about why these birds in particular would make an excellent 'aircraft' for Tian to ride on. What kind of aircraft do they look like?

- In the story the painted cranes 'fluttered off the wall and began to dance... . Everyone was talking about the wonderful dancing cranes.' Cranes are known for their 'dancing'. Find out about the crane dance. You might also like to try 'a crane dance' in your movement lesson.

Language Activities

Tian's Mountain Home

- Think about Tian's lofty mountain home. Explore images (similes) to describe the mountain on which he lived. A simile compares one thing with another, for example: *as high as the sun, as white as a unicorn's back, as cold as a winter's day.*

- String some of your images together to make a picture poem of Tian's home and write your poem in the shape of a mountain. For example:

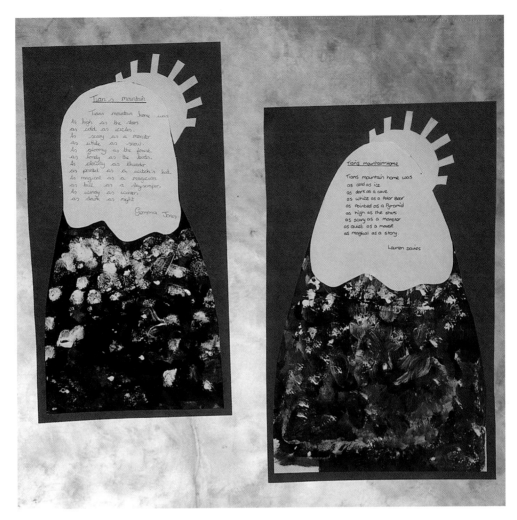

*Tian's mountain home
was as high as the sun,
as cold as a winter's day,
as pointed as a pyramid,
as white as a crane's wing
and as lonely as a planet.*

I Dreamed a Mountain

- Develop your work on similes by writing a poem in three-line stanzas, each first line beginning, 'I dreamed a mountain so moonlit/rocky/high/cold/white/frosty... . The following two lines should then expand the idea. For example:

*I dreamed a mountain so moonlit
it shone like
a Hallowe'en lantern.*

The whole poem should have a dreamy, 'other worldly' feel to it.

City News

- Think of the excitement in the city when people found out about the three dancing cranes at the inn. Imagine that you are a reporter in the local newspaper, *The City News*. Interview the innkeeper to establish the facts, then file a report for the evening newspaper.

Tian's Diary

- Write a diary of Tian's visit to the city as though you were Tian himself. Imagine how he felt as a lonely old man arriving in the noisy city. Give him a date to fly, a date to meet the beggar and exchange clothes, a few days with his begging bowl and so on until at last he returns to his home on top of the mountain. Put your diary into a zigzag book format and illustrate each page.

Flying with the Birds

- In the story Tian and the crane 'flew through the clouds'. Can you find another 'flying' word in the text? Make a thesaurus of words to describe flying, for example, swoop, soar, glide.

- Use some of the words you have found to make up a poem about flying on the wings of a bird. Choose your own favourite birds and follow a simple pattern, for example:

Flying with the Birds
*Swoop through the clouds
on the wings of a swallow.
Soar into the air
on the wings of a dove.
Flutter across rooftops
on the wings of a crane.*

- Imagine flying with the cranes. Find words to describe the feel of the wind in your hair, the sound of flapping wings and the look of the countryside below. For example:

*Between wide white wings,
I travel the morning skies.
The wind sings in my hair,
my cloak flies behind me
and beneath my feet, clouds
float, red in the rising sun.*

- The poems can be written on cloud-shapes and displayed as mobiles.

Chinese Proverbs

- There is a famous Chinese proverb that says, 'A journey of a thousand leagues starts with a single step'. A proverb expresses a truth in a short sentence, so that the words build up a picture in your head, for example: 'Too many cooks spoil the broth'. Can you think of any more sayings like this?

- Listen to the Chinese proverb above and think about Tian's first step and about his long journey (of a thousand leagues?). Try to make up a new proverb for Tian, for example:

Look after others as you have looked after me, or
Great riches start with one bowl of rich soup.

- Write out your proverbs (old and new) in black ink and decorate with Chinese-style writing, and pictures of cranes.

Art Activities

Dancing Crane Wall-hanging

- Take a length of red material as the background for the wall hanging. Outline three cranes on white paper and transfer to silk paper (white for the body and black for the wing feathers). Add details of beaks and legs in felt-tipped pen, then cut out and glue to the red backing and add coloured ribbon. Complete the hanging by gluing wooden dowelling to the top and bottom if desired.

Flying Cranes

- Look for photographs or pictures of cranes. On pale blue backing paper paint a range of snow-capped mountain tops and show the rising sun spreading its light across the sky. Against this background, stick on pictures of cranes in flight with necks outstretched and legs extended (see page 62). Use as a background to display poems of Tian's mountain home from Language Activities.

Tian's Cloak

- Design a richly patterned cloak, such as Tian might have worn, using a wax resist technique. Sketch out the shape of the cloak on white paper. Use a candle or a white wax crayon to draw a Chinese-style design on the cloak. Paint over the design with bright watercolours or poster paints to reveal the wax crayon cloak. Cut out the cloak and hang several cloaks together on a string, as if for sale at a Chinese merchant's stall.

The City Street

- Find pictures of a busy street in China. Look at the curved shapes of the roofs, the Chinese lettering on the shop fronts and the way people are dressed. Use felt-tipped pens to draw your own version of the busy street where Tian sat with his begging bowl as the rich people passed him by.

Rama, Sita and the Demon-king

Once, long ago, a wise and good king ruled the Indian kingdom of Kosala. He had four sons. Prince Rama was his eldest and best-beloved son. One day, Rama married the beautiful princess Sita, and his father promised that, when he died, Rama would inherit the kingdom.

But it was not to be. When Rama's wicked stepmother heard this, she was very angry indeed. "Why Rama?" she shouted. "My son Bharata would make a much better king!" Many years ago, in return for saving his life, the king had promised to grant her one wish, so she said, "My only wish is that you make Bharata your heir and banish Rama and Sita from the palace."

The king had no choice. He knew he had made a solemn promise so, with sadness in his heart, he sent for Rama and Sita and told them to pack up and go and live in a far-off forest, and never to return.

Rama and Sita built a little cottage deep in the forest. They created a lovely garden around it where they grew flowers in summer, and fruit and vegetables in the autumn. Rama went hunting in the forest every day and caught lots of animals and birds to eat, so they never went hungry. They were very happy together in their little cottage and didn't miss life in the palace.

But sometimes Sita felt lonely when Rama was out hunting and she was left alone in the cottage. "I wish I had a pet to keep me company," she said.

One day, Sita saw a beautiful golden deer skipping along the forest track. "Look at that little baby deer, Rama," she said. "I think he must be lost. If only I could have him for a pet, I'd look after him and love him like a child." Rama loved Sita so much that he tried to give her everything she asked for. So he set off to catch the golden deer.

"Be careful, Sita," Rama said every morning as he set off into the forest. "Never open the door to anyone who calls. We still have many enemies who are out to get us." Sita promised to take great care, but one day, while Rama was out hunting, a holy man knocked at the door. He looked so old and ill that Sita felt sorry for him. "Can you spare a bite to eat, my dear?" he asked. Sita invited him in.

However, this was no holy man – it was Ravana, the ten-headed demon-king from the island of Lanka, in disguise. As soon as he was inside the cottage, he changed shape. He grabbed hold of Sita and pushed her roughly into his chariot and said, "If I can make you my bride, I will rule the world!" He laughed a cruel laugh and went off with her. He raced out of the forest, over mountain-tops and across fields until at last they came to the sea. The chariot changed into a giant seabird, which flew across the waves with Sita and Ravana, the demon-king, on its back. Sita was terrified.

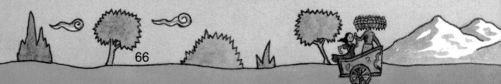

They flew on the seabird's back all the way to the island of Lanka, which was far out in the middle of the ocean. "Never try to escape, young woman," warned the demon-king.

When Rama got home and found Sita gone, he was devastated. He searched all through the forest. Then he called on his friends, the monkeys, to help him. The monkeys looked down from treetops and mountain-tops, but still Sita was nowhere to be found. Next, Rama asked Sampathi, the vulture, to search the skies. When Sampathi got back, he brought bad news. "Ravana, the ten-headed demon, has captured Sita! She is a prisoner on the island of Lanka in the middle of the ocean."

"What shall we do?" said Rama to his friends. "We will never be able to rescue Sita from there!"

Hanuman, the monkey chief, was a son of the wind god. He said, "Leave it to me! I'll soon have Sita home!" He leaped right across the ocean to the island kingdom of Lanka, where the demon-king's palace was studded with so many stolen jewels that it shimmered in the sun. Sita was held prisoner in the palace grounds. She was delighted to see Hanuman and gave him a ring to take back to Rama, so that he would know she was still alive and well. Hanuman said, "Don't worry, Sita. We will soon be able to rescue you."

"Be as quick as you can," she warned. "If I don't marry the demon-king, he says he will eat me for supper!"

When he got back, Hanuman told Rama what he had seen, and showed him the ring, so they quickly gathered an army of bears and monkeys. They built a bridge across the ocean and marched all the way to the island kingdom of Lanka. But the ten-headed demon was waiting for them with a huge army. They fought day and night and many were injured or killed.

Among the wounded, Hanuman saw the injured bodies of both Rama and his brother, Lakshman. He knew that only a magic herb from the mountain could save the brothers so, like a whirlwind, he leapt to the mountain-top to find some. The herb tasted bitter, but Hanuman insisted that they swallow it.

When Rama was well again, he went out on his own to face the demon-king who was a fearsome sight dressed in golden armour with a golden helmet on each of his ten heads. Rama struck him in the heart with a magic arrow and the demon-king fell from his chariot, stone-dead.

Sita came running from Ravana's palace to kiss Rama. Then they rode on the back of a great white swan to be crowned king and queen of Kosala.

Rama, Sita and the Demon-king

Speaking and Listening

- Listen to this story of Rama and Sita read aloud. There are many Hindu tales about Rama and Sita, but this one which tells about their battle with the ten-headed demon-king is perhaps the most famous.

Diwali

- Diwali, or the Festival of Lights, is celebrated by Hindus in honour of Rama. Diwali is an annual festival celebrated throughout India, and in all parts of the world where Hindus live. Find out what Diwali means and how Hindus celebrate it.

Ravana

- Ravana was the name of the ten-headed monster or demon-king who tried to force Sita into marrying him. Diwali is the time when people remember how Rama rescued Sita from Ravana and is celebrated not only as the triumph of light over darkness, but of good over evil. Ravana was able to disguise himself in lots of different ways. How did he disguise himself in the story?

Language Activities

Beginnings

- This story begins with the words, 'Once, long ago, a wise and good king ruled the Indian kingdom of Kosala.' Look for different ways to start the story. You might have said, 'Once upon a time …'. How many other beginnings can you think of to start the story?

A Book about Pets

- Most pet books tell you how to look after cats, dogs, rabbits and hamsters. They give you advice about keeping your pet clean and healthy. They tell you what food is best, the toys they might like to play with and so on. Sometimes the books even give you a list of suitable names. Make a book for Sita, telling her how to look after her pet deer. Remember, this is a magical creature, so you might suggest unusual foods.

Rama and Sita Story

- Write your own version of the Rama and Sita story, paying particular attention to the dialogue, that is, the words that people actually say. Remember all the important events in the story and illustrate the text with appropriate pictures or write the story as a comic strip using speech bubbles.

The Battle of Lanka

- Invent newspaper headlines to describe the Battle of Lanka, for example: *'MONKEYS AND BEARS ADVANCE ON RAVANA'S ARMY'* or *'TEN-HEADED DEMON TAKES ON JUNGLE BEASTS'*. Imagine you are the reporter sent to report on the battle. Describe the noise of the battle, the fearsome sight of Ravana in his golden armour and the feel of the wind as Hanuman leapt to the mountain top.

The Magic Herb

- Hanuman picked a healing herb to make Rama well again. Make up a magic potion recipe for Hanuman to use. Refer to books about herbs to give you ideas, but remember that a magic potion can include lots of imaginary things.

Endings

- The last sentence of the story says, 'Then they rode on the back of a great white swan to be crowned king and queen of Kosala.' Can you continue the story from this point? Write a few sentences to say what might have happened next.

Diwali Acrostic

- Write an acrostic poem about the Diwali festival. Write the word down the left side of your paper and use each letter to start a new line. Think of things that you associate with the celebration and fill in the lines of your poem, for example:

> **D** is for dressing in new clothes
> **I** is for illuminating the house
> **W** is for worshipping Vishnu
> **A** is for approaching with awe
> **L** is for lighting lamps and candles
> **I** is for inviting in a stranger
>
> **DIWALI** is our annual festival of lights.

- Decorate each initial letter of the acrostic in illuminated script.

Riddles

- A riddle is a short poem that both asks a question and hides the answer. Try writing a riddle that describes a character in the Rama and Sita story.

Rama and Sita Flap Book

- Write the Rama and Sita story as a flap book. To make a flap book, you will need two sheets of writing paper, one on top of the other. Begin writing on the top sheet, concentrating on one part of the story only. Ask questions and cut open flaps to reveal illustrated answers on the sheet below. Decorate the story and glue the top sheet over the bottom one.

Art Activities

Diwali Lamps

- Make Diwali oil lamps from clay or salt dough. Mould them with a depression large enough to hold a night-light. When the lamps are dry, paint with pearlised paint and decorate with Indian patterns. Put a night-light inside each.

Demon-king Masks

- Paint and cut out ten demon-king masks, five looking to the left and five to the right. Make them look as fearsome as possible. Put a golden helmet on each of the ten heads. Glue them together in a long row.

Riding on a White Swan

- Create a display of Rama and Sita riding through the streets of Kosala on the back of 'a great white swan'. This should be a very grand picture, full of bright colours. Paint rows of sun-washed houses in the background. Make the swan's curling feathers by twisting white crêpe round a pencil and gluing the overlapping feathers on a white painted swan. Dress Rama and Sita in colourful robes and sit them on top of the swan. (See page 68.)

Book Covers

- Design book covers for the Rama and Sita story. Use coloured card and glue on cut-out individual letters for the title in gold or shimmering paper. Make the covers look very rich, with lots of gold and silver decoration. Add illustrations of Rama and Sita and the great white swan.

For details of further Belair publications,
please write to Libby Masters,
BELAIR PUBLICATIONS LIMITED,
Apex Business Centre,
Boscombe Road, Dunstable, LU5 4RL.

For sales and distribution in North America and South America,
INCENTIVE PUBLICATIONS,
3835 Cleghorn Avenue, Nashville, Tn 37215,
USA.

For sales and distribution in Australia,
EDUCATIONAL SUPPLIES PTY LTD,
8 Cross Street, Brookvale, NSW 2100,
Australia.

For sales and distribution (in other territories),
FOLENS PUBLISHERS,
Apex Business Centre,
Boscombe Road, Dunstable, LU5 4RL,
United Kingdom.
Email: folens@folens.com